THE ANATOMY OF 1

Ribs

Spine
(Vertebrae)

Kidneys

Small
Intestines

Colon

Hip Bone
(Pelvis)

Bladder

Testes

Penis

Tail Bones
(Coccygeal)

Femur

Liver

Stomach

Kneecap
(Patella)

Hindlimb
(Tibia)

Hindlimb
(Fibula)

Metatarsis

Digits
(Phalanges)

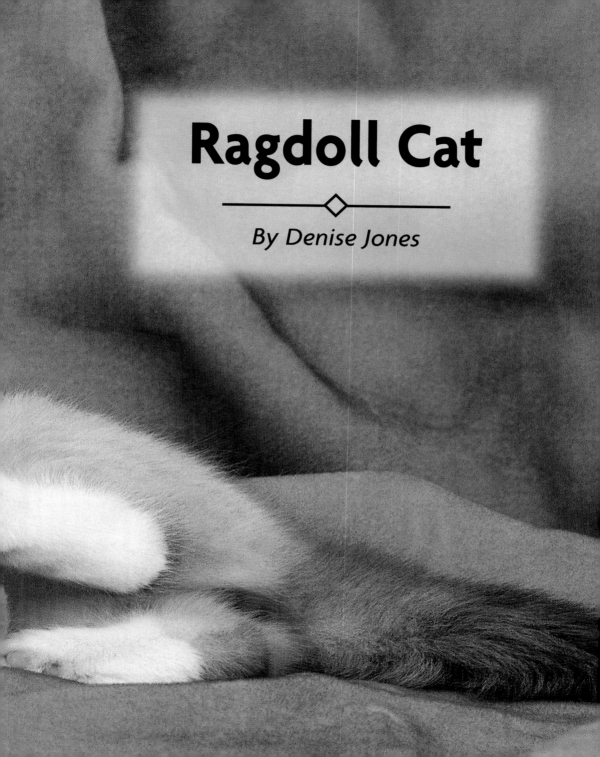

Ragdoll Cat

◇

By Denise Jones

RAGDOLL CAT

CONTENTS

PUBLISHED IN THE UNITED KINGDOM BY:

INTERPET
PUBLISHING

Vincent Lane, Dorking   Surrey RH4 3YX   England

ISBN 1-84286-039-9

Photos by Isabelle Francais and Erin Winters
with additional photos provided by
Michael W. Brim, Cat Fanciers' Association, Carolina Biological Supply, Fleabusters Rx for Fleas, James R Hayden, RPB, Interpet, Dwight R Kuhn, Dr Dennis Kunkel, Phototake, Jean Claude Revy, W B Saunders Company.

The publisher wishes to thank Laura Cure, Chris Gilman, Faye and Maurice LaValley, Dr Gail Lichten, Pat Marengo, Louise Panfile, Suzanne Suraci-Pellegrini and the rest of the owners of cats featured in this book.

Not only is the Ragdoll Cat one of the most beautiful of all cat breeds, but its history is also unique in the cat world.

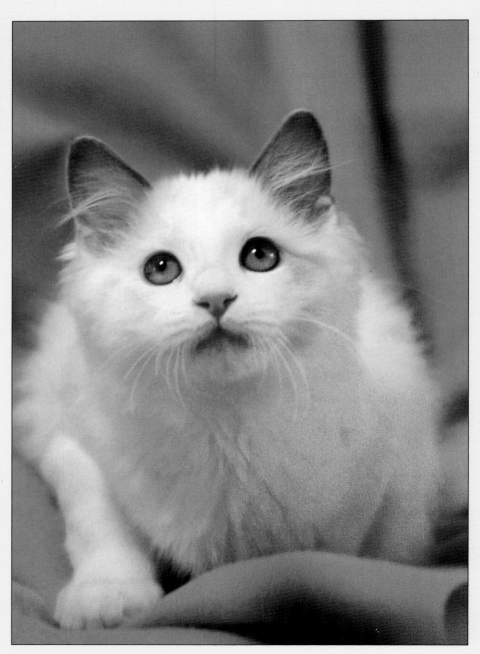

One of the nice things about cats is that many breeds are associated with interesting histories. Some even have fascinating and romantic legends that precede their actual development as a breed. But none quite compare with the history of the Ragdoll. It is not so much the actual development of the breed that was in any way unusual; rather it was the bizarre claims of the breed's founder, Ann Baker. Her statements and promotional methods were, to say the least, most unusual.

No other cat breed was ever developed against such a comparable background. The breed's early history is one of uncertainty with respect to the cats that were part of it. There are numerous versions of both the relationships of the founding cats and of other breeds used in the programme.

The most documented versions are combined here into two summaries. None of the various accounts has been reliably corroborated in detail because the founder's own statements appear to have changed over the years. Also, as time went by, animosity between Ann Baker (the breed's founder) and a number of the people within the breed is evident. This created a situation in which reality, hearsay and accusations on both sides make the truth difficult to establish. For the impartial breed historian, the Ragdoll's early history is a minefield of problems.

JOSEPHINE— THE FOUNDING CAT

The story of the Ragdoll begins with Ann Baker, a breeder of Persians. She lived in the southern Californian city of Riverside. It was the early 1960s. One of Ann Baker's neighbours was a Mrs Pennels, who owned a cat called Blackie. He was apparently a cat of Persian type. Baker often borrowed this cat to mate with her Black Persians. His mother, also owned by the Pennels, was called Josephine. She was a blue-eyed white cat of obvious Angora type. It appears her disposition was not the most amicable that one could wish for.

About 1963 Josephine was involved in a car accident. According to Ann Baker, she was taken to the local university to be treated. Why she was taken to the university and not to a veterinary surgeon remains a mystery; however, following her return to the Pennels' home, she recovered and continued to produce more litters.

Ann Baker noticed that the kittens born after Josephine's accident had unusual characteristics. Unlike their mother, they were extremely friendly and appeared to have a remarkable tolerance for pain. They also had mat-free coats. Further, when picked up they became very floppy—just like a 'ragdoll,' thus the name of the breed chosen by the founder. Baker believed the accident had affected the genetic constitution of Josephine, which accounted for the outstanding characteristics in her offspring. In Baker's opinion, they represented a quirk of Nature. As such, they were worthy of being carefully bred to produce both a beautiful and ultra-docile cat breed. Were it not for the events that were to occur over the following years, Ann Baker, who died in 1997, would be fondly remembered for her diligence in developing a new breed that is today one of the most popular pure-bred cats in the world.

THE FOUNDING CATS
Blackie, already mentioned, had a half-brother who was born after Josephine's accident. Ann Baker called him Raggedy Ann Daddy Warbucks. According to Baker, he was a most impressive cat who looked somewhat similar to the Birman breed. He had a small white blaze, white socks, a white chin, bib and underbelly, as well as a white tip to his tail. Baker started to use this male, as well as Blackie, to mate with her Persians.

Later she acquired two of

RECOGNITION OF THE BREED
The breed gained the benefit of its own club, The British Ragdoll Cat Club, in 1987. This was an important stage in gaining recognition for the breed with Britain's Governing Council of the Cat Fancy (GCCF). In 1990 it gained preliminary status in the Foreign Shorthair group. In 1993 the GCCF created the Semi-Longhair group and the Ragdoll was transferred to this more appropriate group.

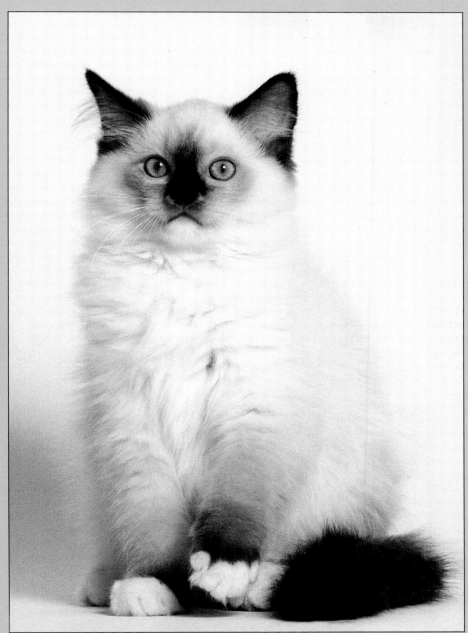

Founder Ann Baker's cats were called Ragdolls because they went limp when picked up, acting just like a ragdoll. However, their popularity was due to their beauty and ability to socialise readily with most humans.

The Turkish Angora may have been involved in the evolution of the Ragdoll.

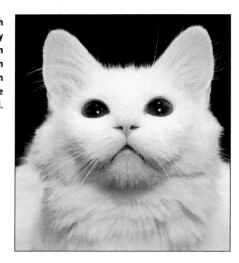

Josephine's female offspring. One was a bicolour sired by Daddy Warbucks and named Raggedy Ann Fugianna. The other, with the name of Buckwheat, was a black female sired by Blackie. It was from these various cats, together with possibly many others that Ann Baker bred from, that the Ragdoll was developed. So ends one account of the initial cats and their relationships.

The second version claims that Josephine was thought to have mated with a black-and-white mitted Longhair. The union resulted in Raggedy Ann Daddy Warbucks, a solid black male, and Raggedy Ann Fugianna, a sealpoint bicolour. In this version Fugianna is a sister of Daddy Warbucks, not his daughter. Daddy Warbucks is

The Ragdoll is quickly becoming more popular than its immediate rival, the Maine Coon Cat.

described as solid black in this version. Another mating of Josephine was with a chocolate Longhair. This resulted in a black-and-white mitted female named Buckwheat. Here Buckwheat is mitted, not a solid black.

Despite these discrepancies, Baker had acquired a small nucleus from which she developed two lines of cats. One was based on Raggedy Ann Fugianna, the other on Buckwheat. A mating between Daddy Warbucks and Fugianna resulted, in 1965, in Raggedy Ann Mitts, Gueber, Kyto and Tiki. Raggedy Ann Kyto and Tiki were the first registered Ragdolls who gained official recognition in that same year with the National Cat Fanciers Association (NCFA), which is no longer operational.

Eventually this line of cats was crossed with that of Buckwheat. From many further matings, the three pattern varieties presently seen in the breed were established. To add further mystery to those early days, it is reported in books and articles that Birmans, Burmese and Persians were also used during the developmental stages.

The use of the Persian would not be surprising, but whether the Birman and Burmese were used is more questionable.

Josephine already carried the white spotting gene needed to create the mitted and bicolour patterns. She may also have carried the recessive Siamese restriction gene needed to create the colourpoint—as might Blackie and Daddy Warbucks. This would remove the genetic necessity to use the two breeds mentioned in the subsequent Ragdoll development programme. Thus ends the early part of the Ragdoll's development.

RAGDOLL MARKETING

With the basis of the breed established, Ann Baker set about

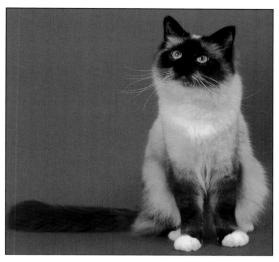

The Birman is frequently compared to the Ragdoll in looks; some authorities claim that the two breeds may be related.

marketing the Ragdoll. She began her promotions with advertisements and articles. She also appeared on local and national TV in respect to her claims that the new breed was somewhat impervious to pain. She would throw a cat in the air to display its docile and floppy nature.

Her claims, from a genetic viewpoint, were quite ridiculous. An accident may damage a cat's physical or mental abilities, but it would not affect the genotype of the individual nor the genetic material it will pass to its offspring. However, there were many people who did not understand this subject, so they were gullible enough to believe what she was saying. As always,

The Burmese is thought to be involved in the history of the Ragdoll, but this is questionable.

when a new pet emerges there is no shortage of those who want to own one for any of various reasons. Some just like to own the latest pet (fashion owners), others see bank notes flitting in front of their eyes at the prospect of breeding and making lots of cash on high-priced kittens. Yet others fall in love with the new breed and just want to be part of its future.

Ann Baker's own ambitions were seemingly to become financially successful with a breed she had created via her own efforts. Also, she clearly believed she needed to retain control over the way in which the Ragdoll would develop as a breed. There is nothing intrinsically wrong with either

of these desires. However, when dealing with a living species it is probably impossible to retain control over its future development for a number of reasons, which are beyond the scope of this chapter to discuss. Nonetheless, Ann Baker tried to do just this.

After the initial recognition by the NCFA she made no further attempts to gain recognition of the Ragdoll within the mainstream of the cat fancy—meaning with the major national registration associations. This would have taken more time and would have meant relinquishing total control over the breed. This apart, her outrageous claims regarding the breed's being

The story of the Ragdoll begins with this breed of cat— the Persian.

Ragdolls usually have a warm, welcoming look, signifying their friendliness.

impervious to pain would have totally alienated her from these associations. Geneticists, vets, indeed anyone who could see the dangerous implications of her claims, all quickly disputed the reality of these. However, as always, this extra promotion only increased interest in the breed.

WILD CLAIMS & DISCONTENT

As time went by, Baker began to make progressively more outrageous claims about the breed. She stated that, while being treated in the local university, Josephine had been subjected to genetic engineering. It was this that had altered her

FRANCHISE AND TRADEMARK

In order to maintain her control over the breed, Ann Baker sold individuals on a franchise basis. Under this arrangement, Baker had control of the breeding policy. She received royalties on each of the kittens sold by those who had bought into the franchise. She also registered the Ragdoll as a patented trademark that was fully enforceable. This meant that if anyone left the franchise, or did not fulfil the terms of the arrangement, he could not market any future kittens as being Ragdolls. In 1971 Baker created her own breed club, the International Ragdoll Cat Association (IRCA), which also operated as a breed registry. Its members were not allowed to exhibit their Ragdolls in shows organised by the major cat associations. The IRCA still remains operational.

genetic make-up; thus, the change in her offspring. Later she stated it was not possible to verify these claims because the procedures were part of a government programme, subject to secrecy. Even later she claimed that Josephine carried human genes, and that her offspring were a link between humans and space aliens.

Not surprisingly, more than a few Ragdoll owners started to distance themselves from her and her association. Some quickly found that their attempts to avoid the terms of their agreement with her resulted in litigation and worry. However, one couple decided to challenge her claim to royalties from kittens produced. They were Laura and Denny Dayton of California.

This couple had obtained a

pair of Ragdolls from Baker in 1969. The cats were Raggedy Ann Buddy (seal colourpoint) and Raggedy Ann Rosie (seal mitted). They became engaged in a protracted legal battle with Ann Baker that was no doubt financially and mentally draining. Yet they stuck to the task and eventually broke the franchise. Other owners were not as willing to battle in court. The Daytons obtained stock from some of these, thus developing a strong breeding nucleus themselves.

Their cattery name was Blossom Time. It became the most commonly seen prefix on pedigrees during the early years of the breed as it became established outside Ann Baker's sphere of influence. The Daytons formed a club called the Ragdoll Society (now the Ragdoll Fanciers Club International) in 1975 and began campaigning with the breed. Today every major association in the world recognises the Ragdoll. The Cat Fanciers' Association (CFA) was the last of the American registries to accept the breed, this being effected in May of 1993.

RAGDOLLS IN BRITAIN

The Ragdoll arrived in Britain in 1981 as a consequence of two friends having seen the breed in American magazines. The ladies

The founder of the breed extricated royalties from all kittens bred and sold under the name of Ragdoll.

were Pat Brownsell and the late Lulu Rowley, who lived in Norfolk. Pat imported a chocolate bicolour male called Blossom Time Proper and the seal colourpoint female Blossom Time Prim. Lulu imported a seal colourpoint male called Blossom Time Lad and a seal mitted female called Blossom Time Lass. These four Ragdolls enabled breeding programmes to commence. Further Blossom Time cats were subsequently added. In due course, other American top lines were also imported, as they are to this day.

THE FAMED TEMPERAMENT

When all the fanciful claims of Ann Baker are removed from the story, there is no denying she did develop a breed with an outstanding temperament, as well as good looks. Clearly those early cats did possess that something extra that enabled the breed to progress even though it was the subject of considerable debate. So how did the breed acquire its fabled unique temperament?

One theory is that Josephine (or one of the cats she was mated to) carried a recessive gene mutation that resulted, when in its double form (one from each parent), in kittens that exhibited a partial sedation of the nervous system. This

THE CRYSTAL PALACE SHOW

On 13 July 1871, an event took place that changed the world of the domestic cat. In the Crystal Palace at Sydenham, London, the world's first all-breed cat show took place. It was organised by Harrison Weir (1824–1906), a noted animal artist and great lover of British Shorthairs.

The success of the cat show saw Weir become a noted cat judge and author. Today he is regarded as the 'father of the cat fancy.' In his later years he complained that Eastern cats were causing the demise of his beloved British Shorthairs. This did not endear him to Persian owners, whose cats were now beginning to dominate the hobby.

The Crystal Palace show attracted thousands of people, many of whom had never seen, or were not even aware of, some of the breed types. On display were many British Shorthairs, Siamese, Manx and a wild cat. Also present was a cat reputed to be direct from Persia. It was said to have a delightful person-ality and its colour was black, grey and white. White Persians were also on view. For many visitors these were by far the most impressive exhibits, with their pale blue eyes and flowing fur.

would give such individuals a more laid-back temperament than is normal within the average cat breed.

It would be very difficult to prove such a theory, but it has the merit of at least being a realistic possibility. Josephine's accident would have had no bearing at all on this gene mutation.

Alternatively, Ann Baker may have been blessed with one or two cats, purely by the random chance of normal gene action, that had outstanding temperaments. Thereafter, by chance or design, she carefully inbred with these in order to increase the homozygosity for this super temperament. To achieve this she would have needed to select for temperament before all else. Thereafter she could give more attention to the appearance of

> ### A SAD ENDING
> Josephine, the mother of the Ragdoll breed, did not live out her life in happy retirement. This would have made a nice fairy tale ending to her role; but, in the real world, things do not always work out that way. It is said that in defending one of her litters from the Pennels' dog, she scratched it. As a consequence, Mr Pennels had her and her kittens destroyed.

her new breed. But paramount to her needs would have been the requirement to apply rigid selection for outstanding temperament at each new generation. Certainly Ann Baker was unique in the cat world. Regardless of all the controversy and animosity she generated, the Ragdoll is undeniably a lasting testimony to what she did actually get right.

Even though Ann Baker suffered a tarnished reputation, there is no doubt that she created the Ragdoll, a variety that has captured the cat world's heart.

A Portrait of the

RAGDOLL CAT

With a weight that can exceed 20 pounds for a male, rather less for a female, the Ragdoll's impression on those seeing it for the first time is one of size. It is one of the largest of all domestic cat breeds, but there is nothing intimidating about the breed. Indeed it exudes an aura of gentle calmness, which gives a strong indication of its underlying temperament. In its mitted variety, which is one of its three pattern types, the Ragdoll is superficially similar to the Birman, to which it may be distantly related.

As with any pure breed of cat, the definitive guide to its conformation and appearance is its official standard of points. A national feline registry, often in association with a national breed club, prepares such a breed 'blueprint.' However, within any country there may be more than one registration association. Each will have its own official standard. The wording of these various standards will be broadly similar, though never an exact duplication of those of other associations.

The following description is not that of any one association. It is a general representation of the breed based on reference to a number of standards. As such, it will meet the needs of most Ragdoll owners. Additional comments are made where these are deemed appropriate, together with basic information on the genetics of the colours and the patterns. Potential breeders and exhibitors should obtain the standard of the association(s) with whom they plan to register their stock.

Always bear in mind that a Ragdoll standard is a general, rather than definitive, guide to the breed. As such, any Ragdoll will appear to meet most of the requirements of the standard. The only way to really appreciate quality is to visit many cat shows and compare the winning cats to the standard. By this method the

Facial markings are identifying characteristics of the Ragdoll.

The Ragdoll eye colour is blue—the deeper the better.

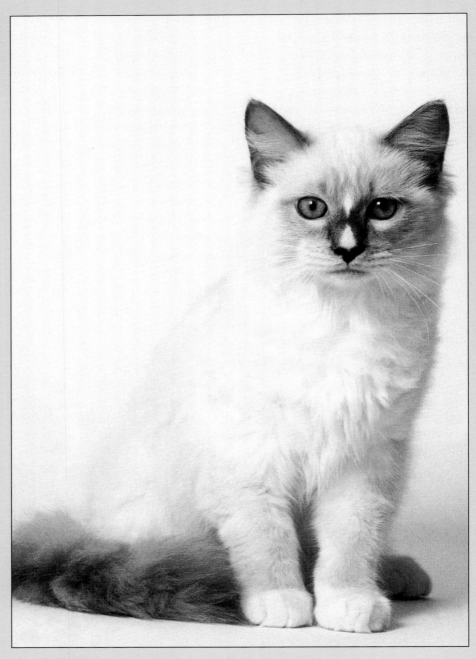

standard becomes more meaningful.

Head: This is broad and of medium size. When viewed from the front, the impression is of a modified wedge with a flat plane between the ears. The cheeks are full and give way to a well-developed and rounded muzzle. The nose is of medium length and displays a slight curve.

The chin is well developed and the teeth should display a level bite. This means the upper and lower incisors should just touch. In profile the head displays a slight curve from the forehead, which then curves gently into the nose. There is no pronounced nose break, meaning an obvious point or 'stop' where the nose meets the forehead.

Ears: Of medium size, the ears are set well apart and exhibit a wide, open base. Their tips are rounded. Viewed in profile they display a slight forward tilt. They are well furnished with hairs near their open base.

Eyes: The eyes should be oval, large and set well apart. The outer edge of the eye should be level with and point towards the ear base. Eye colour is blue, the deeper the better.

Body: The body should be long and muscular, powerfully

built, displaying a broad chest. The shoulders are massive in a mature individual, with the hindquarters being equally so.

Neck: The neck is short and powerful.

Legs & Paws: Legs are of medium length and sizeable bone, in keeping with the substantial body they must support. Medium in length, the rear legs are longer

The Ragdoll head displays a slight curve from the forehead to the nose.

than the front. This will give the backline a slight forward tilt. Paws are large, round, compact and well furnished with hair between the toes. These should comprise five on the front feet and four on the rear.

Tail: This should be long and taper slightly to a rounded tip. As a guide, the length should be at least equal to the distance from the tail root to the shoulders. The tail should be well furred to create the appearance of a generous plume.

Coat: Of good length, its texture is silky and dense, with a minimum of woolly underfur. This creates a relatively non-matting coat. The hair is short on the face but long on the neck, where it forms a definite ruff extending to the bib and upper chest in mature cats. The fur on the front legs is thick, while the rear legs display knickerbockers or britches of good feathery length.

Allowance should be made for seasonal variation of coat length and for the fact that full physical maturity in this breed is not achieved until three to four years of age.

Breed Faults: Head too short, long or narrow. Short nose, Roman nose or one that is straight when seen in profile. Cobby body, overlong body. Fine bones. Eyes round or showing tendency to be Oriental (meaning more almond-shaped than oval). Short legs or tail. Pale eye colour. Coat too short and/or with an unduly heavy woolly undercoat.

COAT PATTERNS
There are three patterns to choose from in the Ragdoll. These are the colourpoint, the mitted and the

The coat of the Ragdoll should be long, silky and dense. A definite ruff is formed around the neck.

COLOURPOINT PATTERN

If you are new to cats you will be familiar with this pattern under the name of Siamese. It is seen in a number of breeds, where it is known as colourpoint or Himalayan so it is not confused with being the Siamese breed. In genetic terms it is created by what is called the Siamese restriction gene.

This pattern is unusual in that it is thermo-sensitive. This means the ambient temperature affects the formation and density of the darker pigment. The consequence of this is that when a colourpointed breed is born, its points are a creamy white. The temperature in the female's womb is too warm to allow pigment to form. Once born, the points become cooler and pigment appears after a few days. In hot climates the pigment will be a little lighter in colour than if the cat lived in a cooler region. Also, as the cat gets older, its pigment will normally become darker. This is because the blood circulation to the points is less efficient than it was when the cat was younger.

bicolour. Most associations, which include both of those in Britain, accept all three. However, the CFA, the largest of the American registries, presently accepts only the bicolour.

COLOURPOINT

The bodily extremities of a cat, meaning its mask, ears, paws and tail, are called its 'points.' In the colourpoint pattern these are a darker colour than the rest of the body. They should be well defined from the body colour. The mask refers to the cheeks, whisker pads, nose, eyes and chin. The nose leather and paw pads of a colourpoint cat should match the colour of the points. A major fault in this pattern would be the appearance of white hairs anywhere in the coat.

MITTED

This variety combines the colourpoint with white. On the face there may or may not be a narrow white blaze, either being acceptable. The chin, bib, chest and the entire underparts to the tail are white. It is a fault if the white from the bib fails to continue in an unbroken manner to the tail. It is also a fault if the chin is not white.

The front paws feature white mittens. These must form a line that does not extend beyond the point where the paw meets the leg. Ideally, both mittens should

The bicolour is the same as the mitted but it has more white, usually with an inverted 'V' on the face.

by symmetrical. It is a fault if the white mittens extend beyond the limits stated. The back legs have white that extends up the legs at least to the hock, and preferably to the level of the underparts. It is a fault if the white fails to reach the hocks. The nose leather colour will match that of the points, while the paw pads will be pink.

BICOLOUR

This variety is the same as the mitted but with the addition of more white. There is an inverted white 'V' on the face. It commences on the forehead and extends down to cover the nose, whisker pads and chin. When viewed from the front, the white of the 'V' must not extend beyond the outer edge of the eye. It should ideally be symmetrical on both sides of the face.

The bib, chest, underparts and front legs should be white. The hind legs should also be white and preferably to the level of the underparts. The nose leather and paw pads are pink. In the European standard of Federation Internationale Feline (FIFe), white

The mitted Ragdolls are typified by these kittens.

spots appearing on the back are acceptable. In the CFA of America standard, pigment spots are allowed on the body while a penny-sized spot on the legs is also acceptable, though not preferred.

The standard of the GCCF of Britain allows evenly distributed patches of white to appear on the back and sides. However, in total these must not exceed one-third of the total back and side areas.

WHITE SPOTTING

In view of its importance to potential breeders, the matter of white spotting, which creates both the mitted and the bicolour patterns, is deserving of comment. Unlike colour genes, the gene creating white spotting is not totally predictable in its action. As such, it is only partly under breeder control. The white spotting gene is a mutation that

A bicolour showing the enchanting blue eyes of the Ragdoll.

prevents the formation of pigment in certain areas of the fur, which is thus white.

Although a mitted or bicolour Ragdoll bred to its own type will create similar offspring, the number of these that would meet exhibition standards would be very variable. Some of a litter may have white where it should not be, others too much white, and yet others not enough. The gene is so variable that its extreme expressions are a white cat with just one pigmented hair to a black cat with just one white hair.

This makes the Ragdoll, and any other breed that has the white spotting gene in its make-up, very frustrating to work with. It is a breed requiring great patience, but when a beautifully marked example appears in a litter it provides an extra special satisfaction compared with that felt when working with predictable patterns.

In respect of the gene's mode of transmission, it has always been regarded in cats as being incompletely dominant. However, some breeders believe it may be recessive, while others think there may be both dominant and recessive genes involved in creating white spotting, and that these have yet to be conclusively identified as such.

Only time and much more

experimental breeding will produce a clearer picture. This may then enable breeders to have more control over the extent of white in the coat. It should be stated that the spotting gene is not the one that creates the all-white cat—though it is capable of creating one in its most extreme expression, as already mentioned.

COLOURS

Presently there are just four colours accepted in this breed. These are traditionally held to be the classic colours of the colourpoint pattern. They are seal, blue, chocolate and lilac.

SEAL

The points should be deep seal brown, which should be of the same shade on all points. The body is beige, which shades to a

A BLUE CAT?

Blue in cats is created by what is called the dilution gene. When this mutation is in double dose (meaning a gene for dilution is inherited from each parent), it causes the pigment to change its density in the hair cells. In effect, pigment clumps and leaves some areas of the cells without pigment. More light is reflected from these pigment-free areas, thus giving the illusion of a colour change.

   The reason it looks bluish is because the seal colour is actually a black that has been degraded very slightly to a dark brown. The dilution gene compacts the brown pigment such that it is again effectively black. The light reflecting from those parts of the cells now without pigment dilutes the appearance of the black to a blue-grey.

The extremes of white facial markings are shown in these two Ragdolls.

1,4   1,6   2,4   3,5   1,6   1,6   3,4   1,4

FROM THE *ATLAS OF FELINE ANATOMY FOR VETERINARIANS* BY HUDSON/HAMILTON, COURTESY OF W B SAUNDERS COMPANY.

PARTICOLOURED CAT

Not a new breed of feline, this 'particoloured cat' illustrates the many possibilities of the feline coat. Since cats come in three basic hair lengths, short, long and rex (curly), all three coat lengths are illustrated here. Additionally, different coat patterns, such as mackerel tabby, Abyssinian and self-coloured, are depicted to demonstrate the differences.

1—3   COAT TYPES
1 Shorthair coat
2 Rex (curly) coat
3 Longhair coat

4—6   COAT COLOUR PATTERNS
4 Mackerel (tabby)
5 Abyssinian
6 Self-coloured

SKIN AND HAIRCOAT OF CATS

Schematic illustration of histologic layers of the integument skin.

A Epidermis
B Dermis
C Subcutis

7 Primary hair
8 Secondary hairs
9 Area of sebaceous gland
10 Apocrine sweat gland
11 M. arrector pili
12 Nerve fibre
13 Cutaneous vessels
14 Tactile hair
15 Fibrous capsule
16 Venous sinus
17 Sensory nerve fibres
18 External root sheath
19 Hair papilla

Schematic illustration of a tactile hair (whisker).

From the Atlas of Feline Anatomy for Veterinarians by Hudson/Hamilton. Courtesy of W B Saunders Company.

THE COLOUR RED

The red colour is created by a dominant gene. This means it cannot be carried in a hidden manner as can the blue, chocolate or lilac. It will also mask the presence of seal. Breeders embracing the red series must be much more aware of the colour genetics of their cats. This will enable colour expectations to be calculated with greater accuracy than if the masked colours are unknown.

lighter colour on the chest and underparts. In some standards the body colour is described as fawn to cream.

BLUE

The points are a bluish grey, which should be of the same shade on all points. The body is a cold-toned bluish white, shading to a lighter colour on the chest and underparts. The term blue in cats is a little misleading. It is more of a slate grey, or smoke, in various depths of shade.

CHOCOLATE

The points are a milk chocolate, which should be of the same shade on all points. The body colour is ivory, shading to a lighter colour on the chest and underparts. This colour is not created by the dilution gene mutation but by one that has a similar effect.

In cats, among the many genes that determine pattern and colour, is one that creates black pigment. Two mutations are known at the black gene locus (the site of a gene on a chromosome). One is for a darkish brown (but lighter than seal) and the other is for a lighter brown. It is the dark one that is called chocolate in colourpoint breeds.

LILAC

The points are a pinkish grey, which should be the same shade on all points. In America the colour is described as a frosty grey with a pinkish tinge. The body is magnolia, shading to a lighter colour on the chest and underparts. The alternative description as used in America is a soft white shading to white. The lilac is created by the action of the dilute gene on chocolate.

NEW COLOURS & PATTERNS

In recent years it has become almost customary for cat breeds to have their traditional colour and pattern range steadily widened. The Ragdoll is no exception. Although the major national registries have not yet standardised the red and cream colours, or the tortoiseshell and tabby patterns, these are recognised by the Ragdoll Fanciers Club International of America. These colours and patterns are available in Britain and will in due course be added to the accepted range already discussed.

In cats, red is a sex-linked colour. The effect of this is that it creates the famed female-only tortoiseshell pattern. In this, red or cream is mixed with any of the accepted colours discussed. When the dilution gene is present in double dose, this creates the cream. If the tortoiseshell pattern is present, this may be in seal, blue, chocolate or lilac. In combination with the dilution gene it creates the blue-cream (blue tortie) and the lilac-cream (cream tortie).

If the tabby pattern (called lynx in America) is present, this faintly overlays whichever other pattern is present. Thus, there is the tabby colourpoint, tabby mitted, tabby bicolour and tortie tabby point, in each of the various colours. It is most evident on the face, which should carry the characteristic tabby 'M' mark on the forehead. Ghost tabby markings may also be seen on the legs and body, to varying individual cat degrees. The addition of the red gene dramatically increases the potential number of colour patterns from which you can choose.

The lilac colour variety should have the same shade on all points and is usually described as a frosty grey with a pinkish tinge.

A HEALTHY KITTEN

Closely inspect any kitten before making a final decision. Keep in mind the following points:

Eyes and nose: Clean and clear with no signs of discharge.

Ears: Fresh smelling and erect.

Coat: Healthy, not dull or dry.

Anal region: Clean with no staining of the fur.

Feet: Four toes on each foot, plus a dewclaw on the inside of each front leg.

Teeth: Correct bite.

There should be no signs of parasites or bald areas of fur. A potbelly may indicate worms.

Given its glamorous appearance, it is no wonder that the Ragdoll is so popular. Before the decision to purchase is made, however, careful consideration should be given to the implications and responsibilities of cat ownership. If more owners would do this, there would be far fewer half-starved pets roaming our streets or having to live in local animal rescue centres.

OWNER RESPONSIBILITY

The initial cost of a Ragdoll represents only a fraction of its lifetime's cost. The first question is, 'Can you afford one?' The kitten needs vaccinations to protect it against various diseases. Boosters are then required every year. Cat food is more costly than that for dogs. There is also the cost of cat litter every week. Periodic vet checks and treatment for illness or accident must be allowed for. When holidays are taken, you may need to board the pet at a cattery.

From the outset there will be additional costs apart from that of the kitten. It will need a basket, carrying box, feeding and grooming utensils, scratching post and maybe a collar and a few toys. If you have any doubts at all about being able to supply all these needs, it is best not to obtain a cat.

Other matters also need careful thought. If you are planning to have a family, will your love for the Ragdoll be compromised once a baby arrives? Cats are generally not a problem with family newcomers providing they are not ignored or treated as being a threat to the baby. Never purchase a kitten for a child unless you want one yourself. If you are elderly, it is only fair to consider what would happen to your cherished pet if it were to outlive you or if you were to become hospitalised for long periods.

It is most unfortunate that many people rush into the purchase of cats on impulse. They then find they cannot cope if problems, and extra costs, ensue. Some lose interest in the pet once it matures past its kitten stage. The evidence of these realities is easily seen in the growing number of cats abandoned or taken to animal shelters every year. Invariably, their owners will make feeble excuses for why the cat cannot be kept. In truth, they did not stop to consider at the outset what responsible ownership entailed.

THE PURCHASING PROCESS

Never rush into the purchase of a companion who is to be given the freedom of your home and will become an integral part of your life. A pure-bred cat may live 20 or more years. This is a long time. It is very prudent to take all those steps that will minimise the chances of your ever regretting the choice you make. Once you have decided on the sex, age, reason for purchase (pet, show or breeding) and desired colour pattern, proceed cautiously, heeding all the advice given here. By following a planned process of selection, you will also gain much useful information.

DOCUMENTATION

When you take delivery of your kitten, certain paperwork should come with it:

1. Three- to five-generation pedigree.
2. Breeder-signed registration application form or change of owner registration form. This assumes the breeder has registered stock. If he has not, the kitten cannot be registered at a later date. It is worth less than the kitten with registration paperwork. You are not recommended to purchase a kitten from unregistered parents.
3. Certificates of health, vaccination and neutering, if this has been effected. Ideally, it is desirable that the kitten's parents have been tested negative for major diseases. Additionally, the breeder should know the blood group of your kitten. This may be of importance at a later date.
4. Details of worming or other treatments attended.
5. Diet sheet, feeding timetable and brand names of food items used. This diet should be maintained for at least ten days while the kitten adjusts to the trauma of moving home.
6. Signed receipt for monies paid.
7. Signed copy of any guarantees. Not all breeders give a guarantee on the reasonable grounds that once the kitten leaves their care its onward well-being is no longer under their control.

Being such a large hefty cat dictates that the Ragdoll is never going to win a feline gold medal in athletics. This very fact, however, makes it ideal for certain types of owner. Not every cat lover wants a curtain-climbing, shelf-jumping express train roaring through the house. There are those who believe that being sedate, serene and well mannered are very important traits in any feline that will share their home for maybe twenty or more years.

Compared to the Siamese, or even the slower British or American Shorthairs, the Ragdoll is ponderous. In other words, its low level of activity and curiosity means it prefers to ponder on things. It is a deep thinker rather than a breed that displays its mental prowess by actually using this to do things! This is not to say a Ragdoll is a static piece of furniture. It has its moments of mischief and high activity, especially as a kitten. But as it matures, it slows down and is quite happy to watch others getting fit—a bit of a 'Garfield' sort of cat.

The Ragdoll generally loves to be handled—though not mauled. It is quite happy to spend its time watching the world go by from a suitable vantage point. Its capacity to get along with other pets, as well as people, make it arguably the ideal cat in these circumstances. Indeed, if its owners are away at work each day, it really should have a companion, such as another cat of a similar nature. When it comes to being a true feline companion for a human, the Ragdoll is among the top cats to choose from. For those already owned by one of these cats, they are the ultimate breed.

KITTEN OR ADULT?

Most potential owners normally want a kitten because it is so cute, cuddly and playful. A kitten is easily trained and has not yet developed bad habits, which the older Ragdoll may have done. This said, if you plan to breed or exhibit, there are advantages in obtaining a young adult. Other potential owners, such as the elderly, may benefit by avoiding the demanding needs of a young kitten. In both these instances, a good age is when the youngster is 9 –15 months old. Even a fully mature Ragdoll may prove an excellent choice for some owners.

Kittens should not be obtained under 12 weeks old, though 14–16 weeks is better. No reputable breeder will sell them younger than this. Less caring breeders will let them go to new homes as young as eight weeks of age. Such juveniles will barely have been weaned. They will not have developed the needed resistance to major diseases. They are more likely to become stressed by the premature removal

ADOPTING AN ADULT

Some owners, such as the elderly, may benefit by adopting an adult cat. They can avoid the demanding needs of a young kitten and enjoy the advantages of a well-trained adult, making grooming an easier task. Breeders and exhibitors can also benefit from purchasing an older cat because it is easier to assess the quality. Sometimes, though, older cats can have bad habits that are hard to break. So if you are thinking about obtaining an older cat, it is important to thoroughly investigate possible behavioural and health problems.

from their mother and siblings. Their vaccinations will not be fully effective. These factors will dramatically increase the risk of immediate problems.

TAKING KITTY HOME

Arrange collection of the kitten as early in the day as possible. If a long journey is involved, be sure to take a few breaks so kitty does not suffer from travel sickness. Do not make stops to show the kitten to friends; this represents a health hazard. Once home, offer the kitten a drink, then allow it to sleep if it so requires. Children must be educated to handle a kitten gently, never to tease it, and to respect its sleeping privacy. Until it is litter-trained, it should be restricted to the kitchen or another room with an easy-to-clean floor surface.

SEX & COLOUR PATTERN

If it is to be purely a pet, the Ragdoll's gender is unimportant. Both are delightful. Males are usually larger, bolder and more outgoing. Females tend to be more discerning about which humans they like. However, each Ragdoll is an individual. Its character and health, more than its sex, should be the basis of selection. Again, the sex is unimportant for the potential exhibitor. It is not even necessary for the cat to be sexually 'entire.' Classes for neuters are featured in shows.

Those with breeding aspirations are advised to obtain only females. All pet owners should regard neutering (males) and spaying (females) as obligatory. Today this can be effected at any age after eight weeks.

The colour pattern is a matter of personal preference. It should never be placed ahead of health and character. Some colours and patterns will be more readily available than others. The more popular varieties may be less costly than the rarer ones. This would generally not apply to prospective breeding or exhibition individuals, where type quality will be as important as colour or pattern.

LOOK BEFORE YOU LEAP

It is important you meet as many Ragdoll breeders and kittens as you can. This gives you a good mental picture of what a healthy typical example should look like and cost for the quality and colour you want. Normally, you will get what you pay for. If you look for the cheapest kitten, there will be a sound reason why it is the cheapest!

The best place to start your search is a cat show. At large cat

Pet shops sell a wide array of scratching posts that are of the highest quality.

Whether you are seeking a pet cat or a show cat, soundness and health are the buyer's first considerations.

shows, most of the colour varieties will be on display. Purchase the show catalogue. It lists all the exhibitors and their addresses. You can see if any live in your immediate locality. Whenever possible, it is best to purchase locally so you can visit the home of the breeder. Some will insist you do so in order to be satisfied that you will make a good owner.

Shows and breeders are advertised in the various cat magazines available from news agents. You can also contact a major cat registry, which will supply a list of national and regional clubs, which are usually able to supply breeder lists. When visiting a breeder, always make an appointment. Try to visit no more than one a day. This reduces the risk you may transport pathogens (disease-causing organisms) from one establishment to the next. Selecting a good breeder is a case of noting the environment in which the cats are kept, the attitude of the owner to you and their cats, and how friendly and healthy the kittens look. It is vital the chosen kitty has an outgoing personality. It must not appear timid or very shy. This indicates a lack of breeder socialisation or a genetic weakness in its temperament. Either way, it is not a kitten you should select.

CHOOSING A KITTEN

If you choose the breeder wisely, and especially if a friend recommends him, this will remove all problems related to your making a poor choice. However, a little knowledge on what to look for will not go amiss. Observe the kittens from a distance to ensure none is unduly lethargic, which is never a good sign. If any kitten displays signs of illness, this should bring to an end any further thoughts of purchase from that source. A reputable breeder would not allow s sickly kitten to remain within its litter.

It is always advisable to select a kitten that shows particular interest in you. Ragdolls are very discerning. If both of you are drawn to each other, this will greatly enhance the bonding essential for a strong relationship.

Once a particular kitten has been selected, it should be given a close physical inspection. The eyes and nose must show no signs of weeping or discharge. The ears will be erect and fresh smelling. The coat should look healthy, never dry and dull. There must be no signs of parasites in the fur. There will be no bald areas of fur, nor bodily swellings or abrasions. Lift the tail and inspect the anal region. This must be clean with no indication of congealed faecal matter. Any staining of the fur indicates current or recent diarrhoea.

Your local pet shop can show you the most suitable litterbox for your cat.

CAT LITTER

The litter that is used in cat boxes can be very variable, and in many cases cats reject the use of a cat box because of the litter. Certainly, if your cat rejects the use of the cat box, you should try different litters. You can start with the litters available at your local pet shop, then you can try sand, dirt, cedar shavings or whatever will appeal to your cat. Several cat owners grow clover in a tray and their cats seem to prefer that. However, the tray is kept outdoors and the cats may simply be marking the clover tray rather than using it for elimination purposes.

The kitten must not display a potbelly. This may indicate worms or other internal disorders. Check the teeth to be sure of a correct bite. Bear in mind that the jawbones do not develop at the same rate. Minor imperfections may correct themselves (they may also get worse), but major faults will not. Inspect the feet to see there are four toes on each, plus a dewclaw on the inside of each front leg.

With respect to the colour, there is no link between this and health other than deafness in certain white varieties. Any faults in the colour or its placement will only be of importance in breeding or exhibition individuals. The potential breeder/exhibitor should obtain a copy of the official standard so they are *au fait* with all colour, pattern and bodily faults of the breed.

KITTY SHOPPING SPREE

Certain accessories should be regarded as obligatory and obtained before the kitten arrives at your home.

Scratching Post

This will save the furniture from being abused! There are many models, some being simple posts, others are combined with play stations and sleeping quarters. These are the best.

Litter Box(es)

Some are open trays; others are domed to provide extra privacy.

Scratching posts are available in many shapes and sizes that are sure to arouse your cat's interest.

Litter-box liners are available to make cleaning your cat's litter box an easier task.

Lightweight collars and leads are available at your local pet shop.

Yet others have special bases in which odour removers are fitted.

CAT LITTER
There are numerous types on the market, each offering advantages and drawbacks. Avoid the low-cost types that contain a lot of dangerous dust. Use those that are fully biodegradable.

Purchase the best quality that you can afford when purchasing items for your cat.

A cat carrying box is an absolute necessity for transporting your pet to the vet. It is also needed if you intend to travel with your Ragdoll.

FOOD/WATER DISHES
Polished metal has the longest wear life. Earthenware is less costly than metal and superior to the plastic types.

GROOMING TOOLS
These will comprise a good-quality bristle brush, a fine-toothed comb, nail trimmers and a soft chamois leather.

CAT COLLAR AND/OR HARNESS
Select elasticised collars. Be sure a name and address disc or barrel is fitted to this. A harness must be a snug but comfortable fit if it is to be effective.

CARRYING BOX
This is essential for transporting the cat to the vet or other places, as well as for home restriction when needed. Be sure it is large enough to accommodate a fully-grown Ragdoll, not just a kitten. The choice is between collapsible models, soft plastic types and, the best choice, those made of wood or fibreglass.

Your local pet shop will have a variety of cat toys with which you can entertain yourself and your cat.

For a kitten, its human environment holds many dangers. Its owner must protect it from these until it becomes agile and wiser. The following dangers lurk in typical households. Always check whether there are additional ones in your home. The most important decision you need to make from the outset is whether or not the kitten is to be given outdoor liberty.

HOW MUCH FREEDOM?

More than at any time in the past the question of how much freedom a cat should be given is the subject of heated debate. It is a very subjective matter. Here the more pertinent points are given so you can relate these to your home location. This, to a very large degree, should influence your decision.

Cats living in or close to an urban area are at the highest safety risk. The amount of traffic is such that death from road accidents is a major concern. In such environments there are high dog populations, some of which are feral. Injury or death from dog attacks is therefore another major source of danger to a feline.

Urban cat populations are also extremely high. Far too many cats are living a virtually feral existence. These are tough, street-wise cats that often carry fleas and other parasites that are vectors of disease. Some will be carriers of, or infected with, feline leukaemia and other deadly diseases.

The typical feline family pet can be badly injured if it becomes engaged in fights with these roaming bullies. Furthermore, their very presence in and around a gentle cat's garden can cause the pet severe stress. This can make it fearful of stepping outside its home.

A washing machine or spin dryer with the door open is a dangerous temptation for kittens; check inside before you use these if the door has been left open.

BE ONE JUMP AHEAD

Seemingly innocuous things, such as doors, can become life-threatening should they suddenly slam shut on a kitten due to a strong draught. When windows and external doors are open, be sure internal doors are secured with a doorstop. At all times be one jump ahead of a kitten in terms of identifying dangerous situations.

THE GARAGE AND SHED

These two buildings are very dangerous for a kitten. Sharp and heavy tools, nails, glass jars, garden weed killers, and open tins of paint are but a sampling of the items the average family uses or stores in these. A kitten may clamber into the engine compartment of a vehicle. This could be fatal if the owner happened to start the engine before the kitten had removed itself. Always know where the kitten is.

Taking these various facts into account, the urban cat is best kept indoors. It can enjoy the benefit of the outdoors if supplied with a roomy aviary-type exercise pen. Some cats can be trained to walk on a lead. This allows outdoor enjoyment, even if this is restricted to the garden. When walking your cat in public places, use only a harness. This is much safer than a collar.

In some instances, it may cause the pet to actually leave its home.

Sadly, if these risks are not enough, there is no shortage of people who will steal a pedigreed cat, the more so if it is friendly. Add to this the number of abusive people who do not like cats roaming into their gardens, and the scenario is not good. Finally, free-roaming cats also take a heavy toll on local bird and wildlife populations.

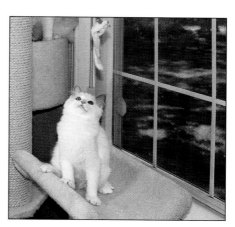

If you set up your Ragdoll's play area near a window, it can enjoy observing the great outdoors.

Inside your home, a Ragdoll kitten is an accident waiting to happen. Without proper training and supervision, cats can usually develop amusing, but dangerous and unsanitary, habits.

THE TRAVELLING CAT

Whenever your cat needs to be taken on a car journey, never let it travel loose in the vehicle, which is illegal. It must always be in its carrying box. If a cat were to go under the clutch or brake pedal when the car was moving, this would be dangerous to all occupants. A cat might also spring from one seat to another, which might distract the driver. This could have disastrous results.

Never leave a cat alone in a car on a hot day. The temperature can rise dramatically to the point that the cat is unable to breathe. It could die of heatstroke. Always leave a window partially open, but not so wide that the agile cat could escape.

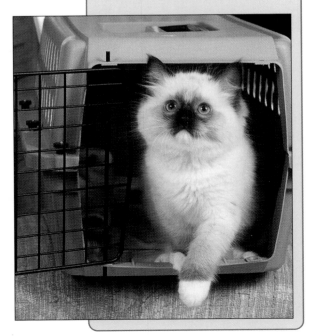

In contrast to urban situations, the cat living in a rural environment is far safer, the more so if there are no immediate neighbours or busy roads. Even so, it is wise to restrict the cat's outdoor freedom to daylight hours. During the night it is more likely to get run over or to threaten local wildlife.

Those living between the extremes of isolated areas and busy urban environments should consider the local risk factor. Generally, it is best to keep the cat indoors but to provide an outdoor exercise pen.

HOUSEHOLD DANGERS

Within its home, a kitten is best viewed as an accident waiting to happen! The most dangerous room is the kitchen. Hot electric hobs, naked flames from gas rings, boiling pans of food or water, and sinks full of water are obvious hazards. An iron left on its board with cable trailing to the floor is an invitation to a kitten to jump up—with potentially fatal consequences. Washing machines or spin dryers with warm clothes in them, and their doors open, are inviting places to nap. Always check the kitty isn't inside if the door has been left open. Cupboards containing poisonous or other dangerous substances should always be kept securely closed.

In the living room the normal dangers are aquariums without hoods, unguarded fires, electric bar heaters, poisonous indoor plants, trailing electrical wires, and ornaments that may be knocked over by a mischievous kitty. Toilets can be fatal to an over-curious kitten. The same is true of a bath containing water. Balconies should be safeguarded to remove the potential for the kitten to slip and fall.

OTHER DANGERS

Other potential dangers are when electric tools are left lying about and connected to power outlets— even worse if they are left on, as with bench saws. If the kitten is given freedom to exercise in a garden containing a pond, the kitten must be under constant supervision. Cherished ornaments should be placed out of reach of the kitten, as much for their safety as to any danger they may present to the kitty. It's not always the direct danger of something that can be the problem. If an ornament or similar item crashes to the floor, this can startle the kitten into a panicked departure! The kitten could then fall from a shelf in its haste.

A Ragdoll can usually find an unsuitable space in which it feels very comfortable.

Today the feeding of cats has been reduced to its most simple level with the availability of many scientifically prepared commercial diets. However, this fact can result in owners becoming casual in their approach to the subject. While the main object of a given diet is to provide the ingredients that promote healthy growth and maximum immunity to disease, it also fulfils an important secondary role.

A proper diet must maintain in the cat a psychological feeling of well-being that avoids nutritionally related stress problems or syndromes. By ensuring the diet is balanced, of good variety and never monotonous, these dual

Cat foods are designed with balanced ingredients with which you can maintain your Ragdoll in excellent condition. Kittens require different diets than mature cats.

roles will be achieved. This approach will also avoid the situation of the cat's becoming a finicky eater.

BALANCE AND VARIETY

A balanced diet means one that contains all of the major ingredients—protein, fats, carbohydrates, vitamins and minerals—in the ratios needed to ensure maximum growth and health. Variety means supplying foods in a range of forms that will maintain and stimulate the cat's interest in its meals. Commercially formulated foods come in three levels of moisture: low, semi-moist and moist (tinned foods).

Generally, the dried and moist forms are the most popular. Dried cat foods have the advantage that they can be left in the cat dish for longer periods of time than tinned foods. They are ideal for supplying on a free-choice basis. Like the tinned varieties, they come in a wide range of popular flavours.

In order to meet the specific needs of a kitten, there are specially formulated foods

MarketPlace: **Ebay**	Order Number: **141825361884-1201248295004**
Order Date: **2015-11-23**	Email: **charonstockton@virginmedia.com**

Items : 1

Item		Locator
Ragdoll Cat (Pet Love)	RY	MUL-2-BD-06-011-38
ISBN : 1842860399		

available. These contain higher protein levels needed by a growing kitten. As it grows, the kitten can be slowly weaned onto the adult types. There are also special brands available from vets for any kitten or cat that may have a dietary problem as well as special diets for the older cat. These may need lower ratios of certain ingredients, such as proteins and sodium, so as to reduce the workload of the liver.

Flavours should be rotated so interest in meals is maintained. This also encourages familiarity with different tastes. Naturally, Ragdolls will display a greater liking for certain flavours and brands than for others.

FRESH FOODS

To add greater variety and interest, there are many fresh foods that Ragdolls enjoy. Some will be very helpful in cleaning

FROM THE ATLAS OF FELINE ANATOMY FOR VETERINARIANS BY HUDSON/HAMILTON, COURTESY OF W B SAUNDERS COMPANY.

MEET THE MEAT-EATERS

Since cats are carnivorous, their teeth are designed to bite and cut. Except for crunching dried foods, cats do very little chewing. They have the fewest teeth of any common domestic mammal—typically 30 (although there are some variations). The canines usually are more developed than the incisors.

DIETARY DIFFERENCES BETWEEN CATS AND DOGS

You should never feed your cat dog food because dogs and cats have different dietary needs. Cats have a much higher need for fats than dogs, and kittens need more than adult cats. Cats also require unusually high levels of dietary protein as compared with those required by dogs. The foods you choose for your cat must supply these essential components.

the teeth and exercising the jaw muscles. All have the benefit of providing different textures and smells that help stimulate the palate. Feed these foods two or three times a week as treats or occasionally as complete meals.

Cooked poultry, including the skin but minus the bones, is usually a favourite, as is quality raw or cooked mincemeat. Cooked beef on the bone gives the cat something to enjoy. Cooked white fish, as well as tinned tuna or sardines, is an example of an ocean delight. Never feed raw fish; this can prove dangerous, even fatal. Although cats rarely enjoy items such as rice, pasta or cooked vegetables, these can nonetheless be finely chopped and mixed with meats or fish. Some Ragdolls may develop a taste for them. Various cheeses and scrambled or boiled eggs will often be appreciated—but never give raw eggs.

If the diet is balanced and varied, the addition of vitamin and mineral supplements is unnecessary and can actually prove dangerous. While certain of

HIGH-QUALITY FOOD

The value of a cat food is determined by its protein/carbohydrate compositions. High-quality foods will contain more protein. The cat is a prime predator and needs a high proportion of protein in its diet.

these compounds are released from the body if in excess, others are not. They are stored and can adversely affect efficient metabolism. If a cat shows loss of condition and disinterest in its food, discuss its diet with a vet.

DRIED FOOD— MORE WATER

If the cat is only given dried foods, it is essential that its water bowl is always full; it will need to drink more. But it is best to give both dried and moist food types. This minimises the risk of urological problems created by pH alkalinity associated with dried diets.

HOW MUCH TO FEED
Food intake is influenced by many factors. These are the cat's age, activity level, the ambient temperature (more is eaten in the colder months), the cat's breeding state (rearing kittens) and the quality of the food. Always follow the breeder's recommendations on diet until your kitten has settled into your home. Thereafter the needed quantity will increase as the kitten gets older, until full maturity at about two or three years of age.

As a basic guide, a four-month-old kitten will require four meals a day. At six months old, one meal can be dropped. By twelve months of age, only two meals will be required, possibly only one if dried foods are also available on a free-choice basis. As the number of meals is decreased, the quantity must be increased.

FOOD AND WATER CONTAINERS

Ragdolls are not too fussy over what vessels are used for supplying their food and water, but a few tips are useful. Ragdolls do not like to eat from dirty dishes any more than you would. The food bowl should be washed after each meal. Water containers should be washed and replenished every day. Saucers make ideal food plates. Wide feeders from your pet shop are

ESTABLISHING DAILY INTAKE
Quoting amounts needed is impossible because of the varying factors mentioned. The best way to establish requirements is on an actual consumption basis. Place a small amount of food on the dish and see how quickly this is eaten. If all is devoured within a few minutes, add a little more. Repeat this until the kitten/cat is satiated and walks away from its dish. Do likewise at the other meals and you will quickly establish daily intake.

excellent for dried biscuits. Pot or polished metal containers are better buys than plastic. They last longer and are easier to keep clean.

WHERE AND WHEN TO FEED

Usually, the best place to feed a cat is in the kitchen. It is important to place food and water dishes as far away from the litter tray as possible. This could otherwise deter the cat from eating. Cats also like to eat in quiet comfort. Meals should be spread across the entire day. When the number is reduced to two, these should be given in the morning and evening at convenient times. For the Ragdoll given outdoor freedom, it is best to feed the main meal in the evening. This encourages it to come home at this time. It can then be kept indoors overnight.

MILK AND CATS
Milk, although associated with cats, is not needed once kittenhood has passed. Indeed, excess milk can create skeletal and other problems. Some cats may become quite ill if given too much. They are unable to digest its lactose content. However, small amounts may be appreciated as a treat. Goat's milk, diluted condensed milk and low-lactose milks are better than cow's milk.

If your Ragdoll's coat is not cared for on a daily basis, it will soon look bedraggled and cause considerable discomfort to your cat. Mats will form that will prevent dead hair from being shed. These will soon enough become entangled with other debris—grass, small sticks, cat litter and even food. It is, therefore, most important that a prospective Ragdoll owner fully accepts that grooming is crucial with this breed. It should never be a chore. If done regularly, it will help bond the cat to its owner. The cat will always be a joy to behold and its owner will be very proud.

Regular grooming also enables close examination of the cat for any signs of problems. These include fleas or mites, small wounds, abrasions, swellings and bald areas. The grooming process should include inspection of the cat's ears, eyes, teeth and nails.

Always purchase the best-quality items. Avoid the use of low-cost plastic-toothed combs and brushes. These create static electricity. This results in fly-away and crinkled hair that is not the best state for this breed's coat.

Before we discuss grooming procedures, a few general points should be made. If grooming is not to be reduced to a battle between cat and owner, it is essential the kitten finds this a pleasurable experience. This will not be the case if the owner is heavy-handed in his or her use of the brush, and more especially the comb. The most tender parts of the cat are its underbody parts and tail. These must be groomed with this fact always in mind, doubly so if tags have formed.

Some owners groom the cat on their laps, others on tables. This author prefers a table. Ensure the surface is of a non-slip type—a rubber mat is recommended for

Your Ragdoll requires daily brushing to maintain its coat in good condition.

this purpose. Again, some owners will commence with the comb, but it is better to use the brush first. It is more forgiving, thus gentle. It avoids unnecessary pulling of the hair.

BRUSHING
Commence on the neck and brush down the fur to the tail. This will remove any small bits of detritus in the coat. Next, brush down the chest, body sides and flanks. With the kitten now familiar with the feel of the brush, gently turn and secure the kitty on its back while its belly is brushed. Groom the tail by forming a parting with the brush and grooming the fur at right angles.

This completed, brush against the lie of the fur. Begin on the neck and brush a few inches at a time, working around the body as before. As each small area is commenced, a little baby powder can be sprinkled around the hair roots. As this is brushed and combed out, it will clean the fur, remove grease and help to keep it tag-free. Talcum powder can be used, but it may cause irritation. Powdered chalk is another long-established alternative.

Finish by brushing with the lie: the hair should then be tag-free. Now combing will be easier. A tip for show-cat owners is that the use of powder in the coat is most advantageous in the lighter coat colours. Use powder

HAIRBALLS (Trichobezoar)
When cats self-groom, they invariably swallow some of their hairs. Normally these do not create a problem. However, if many dead hairs are in the coat, these may be licked and swallowed to accumulate in the stomach as hairballs. These are more common in longhaired breeds than in those with short hair. Hairballs may create intestinal blockages which may so irritate the cat's intestinal tract that it vomits the hairball or voids it via its faecal matter.

If the hairball is not removed, and the cat displays reduced appetite, veterinary assistance is needed. Regular grooming greatly reduces the risk of this condition. Additionally, a teaspoon of liquid paraffin or other laxative once a week may be helpful in cats prone to this problem, but it is unlikely to remove an existing hairball. Pineapple juice containing the enzyme bromelain may break down small furballs. One teaspoonful a day for three days is the recommended dosage.

GROOMING EQUIPMENT

The following will be required for complete grooming:

1. Round-ended, cushioned pin brush
2. Bristle brush
3. Medium-toothed metal comb with handle
4. Flea comb
5. A pair of guillotine nail clippers
6. Powder (If the cat is dark coloured and required for exhibition, a soft chamois leather is useful.)
7. Supply of cotton wool and cotton buds
8. Plastic pouring jug
9. Spray attachment for taps
10. Cat shampoo (Those for dogs are not suitable for felines. A baby shampoo can be used but is not as effective as one formulated for cats.)
11. One or two quality towels
12. Good hair dryer (the quieter the better)
13. Non-slip rubber mat
14. Good-sized plastic bowl with a rubber mat placed inside (to use as bath if sink is not suitable)
15. Medium-soft toothbrush and feline toothpaste (A saline solution is an alternative, but less tasty.)
16. An appropriately sized plastic or other container in which to keep kitty's boutique apparel

From the Atlas of Feline Anatomy for Veterinarians by Hudson/Hamilton. Courtesy of W B Saunders Company

DECLAWING

Declawing is the surgical removal of all of the claw (or nail) and the first toe joint. This practice is heavily frowned upon and even illegal in some countries, such as the United Kingdom.

Unfortunately, in some areas of the world this procedure is still performed. Some owners only have the claws from the front feet removed; others do all four feet. An alternative surgical procedure is removing the tendon that allows the cat to protract its claws. This procedure, referred to as a tendonectomy, as compared to an onychectomy (removal of the claws), is less traumatic for the cat. Claws still must be filed and trimmed after a tendonectomy.

Declawing is not always 100% successful. In two-thirds of the cases, the cats recovered in 72 hours. Only 4–5% of the cats hadn't recovered within a fortnight. About 3% of the cats had their claws grow back!

Ragdoll kittens should be brushed daily so they will become accustomed to the grooming routine.

CLEAN CATS

Cats are self groomers. They use their barbed tongue and front paws for grooming. Some cats never groom themselves, while others spend up to a third of their waking hours grooming themselves. Licking stimulates certain skin glands that make the coat waterproof.

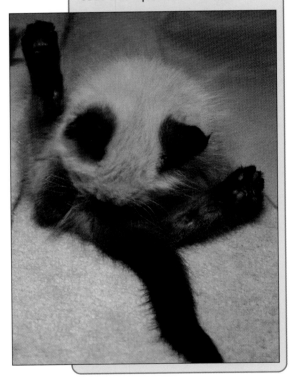

COMBING

Combing should be done in the same manner as the brushing, except that the final comb need not be done with the lie in most varieties. Combing against the lie is a good opportunity to see if there are any parasites present. These often favour the tail base or the neck behind the ears. If any mats should be found in the coat, these must be teased out using the index finger and thumb of both hands. Be very careful not to pull away from the skin while doing this. It will be painful and the cat will object. Never bath a cat that has even the smallest of mats in its fur. Once soaked, these will shrink into tight balls that will be much harder to tease apart.

BATHING

During the course of its life, there will usually be a number of occasions when any cat will need a bath, this being more so for a longhaired breed. For the Ragdoll show cat, this will normally be a

sparingly in the darker ones. The chamois leather is better to polish the darker coat. It produces a better shine than if excess powder has been used.

PRESS-ON NAILS!

A stylish and fairly successful inhibitor of scratching is a plastic covering on the nails. A plastic sheath is placed over each nail and glued on with a strong, permanent adhesive. Depending upon the cat's activity, these sheaths last from one to three months.

HAIR GROWTH

Cat's body hairs grow from the follicles, which are connected to the dermis. Tactile hairs (whiskers) are thicker and longer, originating three times deeper than the normal body hairs.

necessity about seven days prior to a show.

Using the kitchen sink is preferable to a bath. This saves bending and allows for better control of the cat. To prevent the cat from sliding, use a rubber mat. A spray attachment is more efficient than a jug to wet and rinse the coat. The cat should have its own towels.

The choice of shampoo is important. It should ideally be formulated for cats—do not use one for dogs. This could cause problems on a cat's coat. Baby shampoos are the best alternative. Dry shampoos in powder form are available from pet shops. Alternatives would be talcum powder, powdered chalk or heated bran flakes.

The kitten should be bathed by the time it is six months of age. This will familiarise it with the process before it matures and the process degenerates into a pitched battle. Cats have no love of bathing but can come to accept it if it does not become an unpleasant ordeal.

Grooming should always precede bathing, as this will remove any dead hairs. The key to success lies in ensuring that no water or shampoo is allowed to enter and irritate the eyes or ears. You should be able to cope single-handedly with a kitten. However, it may be prudent to have someone else present just in case the adult proves more of a super cat than a kitten!

HAIR, HAIR EVERYWHERE

Cat's hairs grow denser on the abdomen than on the back. The hairs grow according to both light periodicity (daylight versus dark nights) and temperature. Outdoor cats living in colder climates cast their coats twice a year, in the spring and fall, while house cats do so all year long.

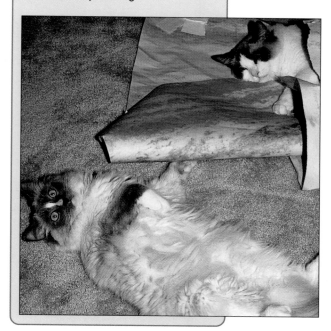

The water temperature should be warm, never cold nor too hot. Prepare a shampoo and water solution before commencing. Have a large towel at hand. Start by soaking the fur of the neck, then work along the back, sides, legs and tail. Pour shampoo onto the back and work this in all directions until the cat has been fully shampooed. Next, thoroughly rinse all the shampoo away. It is essential that none be left in the coat, otherwise it may cause later irritation. The use of a hair conditioner is optional. Its main drawback is that it may make the coat too greasy within days of the bath. Gently but firmly squeeze all water from the coat. The face can be cleaned using a dampened flannel.

Give the cat a brisk rubbing to remove as much liquid as possible from the coat. Now the dryer can be used. Be very careful not to hold this too close to the fur,

Using a kitchen sink when bathing your Ragdoll allows for better control of the cat.

DRY SHAMPOO

A dry bath may be preferred to a wet one during very cold weather or when the cat is not well enough for a water bath. Sprinkle dry shampoo into the coat and give it a good brushing. This will remove excess grease and dirt without being as thorough as a wet bath. Be very sure all the powder is brushed from the fur to avoid potential irritation and consequential scratching.

otherwise it may burn the skin. Keep the nozzle on the move continually. While drying, it is best to be grooming the coat at the same time. This will need the help of another family member to hold the cat while you dry and groom. If the drying process is done correctly, the cat will actually enjoy this part of its grooming once familiar with it.

When the cat is dry, it should be given a final good brushing, then kept indoors for a couple of hours to ensure it is thoroughly dry. Baby powder can be used before the final brushing. Your Ragdoll will now look and smell magnificent.

EARS, EYES AND NAILS

When inspecting the ears, look for any signs of dirt. This can be gently wiped away using a dampened cotton bud or one with just a little baby or vegetable oil on it. Never

FROM THE ATLAS OF FELINE ANATOMY FOR VETERINARIANS BY HUDSON/HAMILTON. COURTESY OF W B SAUNDERS COMPANY.

Never attempt to probe into your Ragdoll's ear. It is extremely dangerous, especially if the cat flinches or suddenly jerks its head.

CAT COATS

The long primary hairs of longhaired cats can be almost three times as long as those of a shorthaired cat. The genes for length of hair are independent of the genes for colour. The original colour of cats is the mackerel or tiger-striped pattern. This pattern was inherited from the ancestors of the house cat.

RETRACTABLE CLAWS

When at rest, a cat's claws are retracted. The muscles hold the claws in their sheaths. The claw is then extended if the cat wishes to attack prey, defend itself, grab an object or climb. That is why your cat's claws are not always visible. This is true for all species of felines except the cheetah, which is unable to retract its claws, except when it is very young.

attempt to probe into the ear. If the ear is very waxed, this may indicate any of various health problems. A visit to the vet is recommended. The corners of the eyes can be gently wiped with damp cotton wool to remove any dust that occasionally accumulates.

Inspection of a cat's claws is achieved by firstly restraining

GINGIVITIS
(Plasmocytic-Lymphocytic Stomatitis)

There are many causes of this condition. But the end result is the same—bad breath, excessive plaque, tooth loss and, almost certainly, pain. The cat salivates excessively, starts to eat less and consequently loses weight. On inspection, the gums are swollen, especially in the area of the premolar and molar teeth, and bleed easily. There are various treatments, such as antibiotics, immunostimulants and disinfectant mouth gels. However, these invariably prove short-term relief and merely delay the inevitable treatment of extraction.

Prevention avoids this painful condition. Regular tooth inspection and cleaning, plus provision of hard-food items, such as cat biscuits, achieve this to a large extent. There are also special cat chews made of dried fish that help clean the teeth. They also contain antibacterial enzymes that minimise or prevent secondary bacteria from accumulating. Ask for these at your pet shop or vet's surgery. Gingivitis may commence in kittens, so do not think it is something that only occurs in the older cat.

TEETH

From its youngest days, your kitten should become familiar with having its teeth cleaned. Many owners do not give the cat's teeth the attention they should. This has become progressively more important due to the soft diet regimens of modern cats. Initially, gently rub the kitten's teeth using a soft cloth on which toothpaste has been placed. This will accustom the kitten to having its teeth touched as well as to the taste of the tooth cleaner. When this is no problem for the kitten, you can progress to a soft toothbrush and ultimately one of medium hardness. Periodically let your vet check the cat's mouth.

Introduce the Ragdoll kitten to tooth cleaning at a young age.

the cat while on its back on your lap or held against your chest. Hold the paw and apply pressure to the top of this with your thumb. The nail will appear from its sheath. If the nail needs trimming, use the appropriate trimmers.

It is vital you do not cut into, or even too close to, the quick, which is a blood vessel. This can be seen as a darker area of the nail in pink-clawed cats. It is more difficult, or not possible, to see the quick in dark-coloured nails. In such instances, trim less. You may need a helper to do the trimming or the holding. If in doubt, let your vet do this for you. If cats have ample access to scratching posts, they will only infrequently, if ever, require their nails to be trimmed.

Clipping your Ragdoll's nails isn't too difficult if the kitten has become accustomed to the procedure.

One of the outstanding virtues of cats is that they are easy to live with. They are fastidious in their personal habits related to grooming and toilet routines and basically require very little of their owners. Nonetheless, behavioural problems in cats can occur, and an owner needs to understand all the possible causes and solutions. You may never encounter a single problem with your cat, but it pays to be prepared should your feline charge disrupt your domestic bliss.

WHY WHISKERS?

Cats are famous for their whiskers. The whiskers are tactile hairs by which cats feel. Most tactile hairs are on the cat's face, mostly on the upper lip and around the eyes and the wrist (carpus). These carpal hairs are extremely sensitive and are found on many predatory animals that use their front paws for holding their victims.

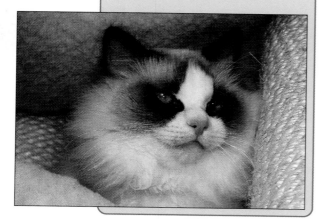

THE BASIS OF TRAINING

The most effective means of training a cat is via reinforcement of success. A cat learning from lavish praise of doing what is required will want to repeat the action to gain more affection. There are no potential negative side effects. Conversely, when scolding or another method of discipline is used, there is always the possibility that the cat will not relate the punishment to what the owner had intended.

For example, you cannot discipline for something done in the past. The past is anything much longer than a few minutes ago. If you call the cat to you and punish it for something done hours earlier, it cannot relate to that action. It will relate the discipline to the act of going to you when called! This will create insecurity in the pet, increasing the risk that more problems will develop.

REMEDIAL METHODS

When faced with a problem, firstly try to pinpoint the likely cause(s). Next, consider the remedial options. Be sure these

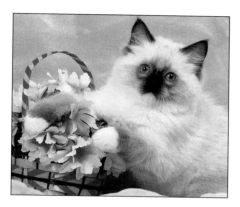

The key to a sweet kitten is early training.

will not result in negative side effects linked to you. Always be the paragon of patience. Some problems may be extremely complex and deeply rooted within the cat's behaviour patterns. As such, they are habits not easily changed and often difficult to analyse. In discussing the following problems, it is hoped you will understand the basic ways to correct other unwanted

SETTING THE GROUND RULES

From the outset you must determine the ground rules and stick to them. Always remember that your companion's patterns of behaviour begin to form from the moment it first arrives at your home. If the future adult is not to be given outdoor freedom, then do not let it outdoors as a kitten. If any rooms are to be out of bounds to the adult, then do not let the kitten into them. Stability is vital in a cat's life; without it, the result will be stress and its related behavioural changes.

Ground rules of how to handle the kitten and to respect its privacy when sleeping should be instilled into all children. The cat's meals should be given at about the same time each day. This will have the secondary advantage that the pet's toilet habits will be more predictable.

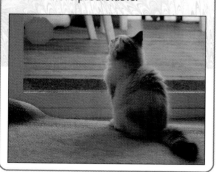

THE TRUTH ABOUT CATS AND DOGS

Cats are unique in having the scrotum fully haired, a marked difference from their canine counterparts. This led one keen observer to say that cats were not small dogs! Dogs were domesticated well before cats since cats only served to protect the abode of the owner from rodents, while dogs served as guards, hunters, herders, exterminators and as loyal companions that were readily trainable. Cats have always been more independent and less trainable.

POSSIBLE CAUSES OF LITTER-BOX PROBLEMS

1. The litter tray is dirty. Cats never like to use a previously fouled tray.
2. The litter has been changed to one of a different texture that the cat does not like. Generally the finer-grained litters are the most favoured.
3. A scented litter is being used to mask odours. The cat may not like the scent. Such litters should not be necessary if the tray is regularly cleaned.
4. The tray is regularly cleaned, but an ammonium or pine-based disinfectant is being used. This may aggravate the cat's sensitive nasal mucous membranes. Additionally, the phenols in pine are dangerous to cats.
5. The litter tray is located too close to the cat's food and water bowls. Cats do not like to eat near litter trays or to defecate/urinate close to their feeding area.

6. Another cat or free-roaming pet has been added to the household and is causing the cat stress. In multi-cat households, two or more trays may be needed.
7. There is insufficient litter in the tray. There should be about 1 to 2 inches of litter depth.
8. The cat has developed a fear of using the tray due to an upsetting experience. For instance, the owner may have caught the cat as it finished using the tray in order that it could be given a medicine. Children may be disturbing it while it is relieving itself.
9. The cat is ill (or elderly) and is unable to control its bowel movements. Veterinary attention is required.
10. The cat, because of one or more of the previous problems, has established other more favourable areas.

patterns of behaviour that might occur. But always remember it is far better to avoid a problem than correct it.

THE LITTER TRAY

A very common problem for some owners is that their cat starts to attend to its toileting needs anywhere other than in its litter tray. The problem may become apparent from the time the kitten gets to its new home, or it may develop at any time during its life. So, let us start from the beginning and try and avoid the situation.

Until you are satisfied the kitten is using its litter tray, do not give it access to carpeted rooms. The youngster should already have been litter-trained well before you obtained it. You should buy a litter tray similar to the one it is already familiar with. It is also important that the same brand of litter is used, at least initially. Place the tray in a quiet spot so the kitten has privacy when attending to its needs.

A kitten will need to relieve

itself shortly after it has eaten, exercised or been sleeping. Watch it carefully at these times. If it stoops to attend to its needs other than in the litter tray, calmly lift it into its tray and scratch at the litter. Never shout or panic the kitty by making a sudden rush for it. If it does what is hoped, give it lots of praise. If it steps out of the tray, gently place it back in for a few seconds.

If nothing happens, be patient and wait, then repeat the process. If it fouls the kitchen floor when you are not watching, simply clean this up and wait for the next opportunity to transport the kitten to its tray. It rarely takes long for a kitten to consistently use this. Be very sure the tray is kept spotless. Cats have no more desire to use a fouled toilet than you do. Every few days give the cat tray a good wash using soapy water and always rinse it thoroughly. Allow it to dry, and then fill the tray with litter to depth of about one to two inches.

By identifying the cause(s) of litter-box problems, the correction is often self-evident. However, once the cause has been corrected, this is only part of the solution. Next, the habit of fouling other places must be overcome. Where possible, do not let the cat enter rooms it has started to foul until the odour has had time to fully disperse. Wash the area of the fouling. Then treat carpets and

CAUSES OF SCENT MARKING

1. Another cat, or pet, has been introduced to the household. It may be bullying the resident cat. This problem may resolve itself when the two get to know each other. The more cats there are, the longer it may take for the situation to be resolved. Much will depend on the space within which the cats may roam and whether they are able to avoid those they dislike.
2. The birth of a new family member may annoy the cat for a while, especially if its owner suddenly gives it less attention.
3. A friend staying in the home for a few days may not like cats. If 'shooed' away a number of times, the cat may feel it should assert its position and mark it.
4. If the cat is given outdoor freedom, a bully may have moved into the territory. Having lost control of its own garden, the pet may assert its territorial boundaries within its home. If a cat flap is used, another cat may be entering the home and this will trigger the resident to scent mark.

SCRATCHING FURNITURE

All cats need to scratch in order to maintain their claws in good condition. For this reason, one or more scratching posts strategically placed in the cat's most-used rooms will normally prevent the problem. Place the post in front of the scratched furniture. It can be moved steadily further away once the furniture is ignored. This is a problem that may become more manifest when cats are not allowed outdoors and have insufficient indoor opportunity to scratch.

soft furnishings with an odour neutraliser (not an air freshener) from your pet shop or vet.

If the cat cannot be prevented from entering certain rooms, then cover previously fouled areas with plastic sheeting or tinfoil, or rinse the fouled area with white vinegar (which cats hate!). Also, place a litter tray in the fouled room while the retraining is underway. It may help if a different size, type or colour of tray is used.

THE PICA SYNDROME

The term 'pica' is a veterinary term that refers to a morbid desire to ingest things that are abnormal to the cat's diet. Cats are often addicted to soft materials like wool, silk, cotton or a mixture of these and synthetic cloths. Hard plastics, wood and even metals have been involved in this pica syndrome. If you observe your cat chewing these fabrics or materials, speak to your vet. Most vets who observe the pica syndrome think it is a nervous problem that can successfully be treated with drugs normally used for depression. In any case, the genetic makeup of your cat should be investigated and if pica occurs in any of the parents or previous offspring, do not breed your cat.

SCENT MARKING

Both sexes scent mark, though males are more prolific. It is a means of advertising their presence in a territory, thus an integral part of their natural behaviour. Spraying is usually done against a vertical surface. It tells other males that the individual is residing in that territory. Alternatively it will tell a female that a male lives close by—or it will tell the male that a female is in the area. It is thus a very important part of a cat's social language.

Neutered cats have little need to mark their territory or leave their 'calling' card to attract mates. They are far less likely to spray than those not altered. However, scent marking may commence when the cat is attempting to assert its position in the household.

To overcome the problem of scent marking, you first need to try and identify if there is an obvious specific cause. In multi-cat households, it also requires positive identification of the sprayer(s) and the favoured spraying surface. Giving the cat more freedom and its own sleeping place if it does not have one may help. Covering the sprayed surface with plastic sheeting, or a cloth impregnated with a scent the cat does not like (such as lemon, pepper or bleach), may be successful. Spraying the

CAT SCRATCH DISEASE

An objectionable habit of many poorly raised kittens is their exuberant jumping to greet you. This flying jump may result in the kitten being attached to your body; otherwise it will fall to the floor and may injure itself. In the attachment process, your skin will usually be pierced and this is a health concern. All cat scratches and bites should be thoroughly cleaned with an antiseptic soap. If a sore appears at the site of the wound, you should visit your family doctor immediately.

Cat scratch disease is a well-known problem. It is caused by a bacterium *(Rochalimaea henselae)* that is usually easily treated with antibiotics. However, more and more cases show resistance to the usual antibiotics.

Untreated cat scratch fever may result in an enlargement of the lymph nodes, imitating a cancerous condition known as lymphoma. Interestingly enough, the lymph nodes, upon biopsy, may show large Reid-Sternberg cells, which are a characteristic of Hodgkins lymphoma. The bottom line is that cat scratches should be taken seriously.

MAN MEETS CAT

Early man, perhaps 8000 years ago, started his symbiotic relationship with domestic cats, *Felis catus* or *Felis domesticus*. The cats killed and ate the rats and mice, and probably anything else which crawled and was small, which early man attracted and considered as pests. Early man reciprocated by allowing the cat to sleep in his cave, hut or tent. Cats, being essentially nocturnal, kept the small mammals (rats, mice, etc.) from disturbing the sleep of early man.

As early man evolved to modern man, the domestic cat came along as an aid to pest control. This was especially true of peoples who farmed, as farmers were plagued with rodents. Though most cats were not selectively bred for their predatory skills, it was obvious that those cats that were the best hunters were more successful in evolutionary terms than the cats that were more meek. Modern cats have changed very little from the cats from which they descended. There are still, today, cats that are very predatory, attacking small mammals and birds; there are also meek cats which, unless fed by their owners, would perish in a competitive cat society.

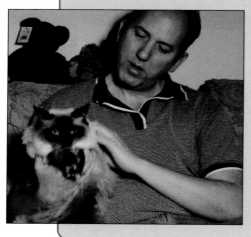

It has been shown repeatedly that if kittens are socialised in a proper manner, they will become peaceful pets. This includes lions and tigers. If the kittens are not socialised properly, they revert immediately to their aggressive predatory behaviours.

cat with a water pistol when catching it in the action is a common ploy. Veterinary treatment with the hormone progesterone may prove effective—discuss this with your vet.

SCRATCHING

Scratching is a normal feline characteristic. Unfortunately, house cats tend to destroy the furniture to satisfy their need to scratch. Feral or outdoor cats usually attack a tree because trees are readily accessible and the bark of the tree suits their needs perfectly. If the outdoor cat lives in a pride, it will scratch more than a solitary feral cat. The reasons for this are known. When cats scratch, they leave telltale marks. Parts of the nail's sheath exudate from glands located between their claws and the visual aspects are the marks that cats leave to impress or advertise their presence.

Cat owners whose cats scratch should not consider the scratching as an aggressive behavioural disorder. It is normal for cats to scratch. Keeping your cat's claws clipped or filed so they are as short as possible without causing bleeding may inhibit scratching. Your vet can teach you how to do this. Clipping and filing should be started when the kitten is very young. Starting this when the cat has matured is much more difficult and may even be dangerous.

There are ways to control annoying cat scratching. Certainly, the easiest way is to present your cat with an acceptable cat scratching post. These are usually available at most local pet shops. The post should be covered with a material that is to your cat's liking. If your cat has already indicated what it likes to scratch, it usually is a good idea to cover the post with this same material. Veterinary surgeons often suggest that you use sandpaper, as this will reduce the cat's nails quickly and it will not have the urge to scratch. Certainly using hemp, carpeting, cotton towelling or bark is worth a try. Once the cat uses the post, it usually will have neither a desire nor a need to scratch any place else.

Besides the physical need to scratch, many cats have a

FERAL CATS

Free-roaming, near-wild cats are, as a general rule, undernourished. They spend most of their time searching for food. Consequently, those feral cats that have kittens spend less time with their kittens than well-nourished cats. It has been shown that kittens born to feral mothers are usually unsocial and show little affection for their mothers. Obviously, they would show a similar lack of affection for a human. That's one of the reasons that feral kittens make poor pets and should neither be adopted nor brought into your home. Kittens, which for any reason are separated from their mothers at the age of two weeks, develop an attitude of fear and wariness. They shun contact with other cats or humans and can even be dangerous if they feel trapped.

psychological need to scratch. This is evidenced by where they scratch versus what they scratch. Often cats prefer semi-darkness. Some prefer flat surfaces and not

TIDY TOILETING

During the kitten's stay in the nest box, the mother will assist or even stimulate bowel and urine elimination, at least for the first month of the kitten's life. The mother also does the clean-up work in the nest box. But once the kitten is older, it becomes capable of relieving itself out of the nest box. Usually the kitten likes sand, soft earth or something that seems absorbent and is easily moved with its paws. By the time the kitten is two months old, it should develop the discipline of covering its elimination. Not all kittens develop this discipline, though the use of an absorbent clay litter seems to be helpful in developing this discipline in young cats. Your local pet shop will have various cat litters to offer you.

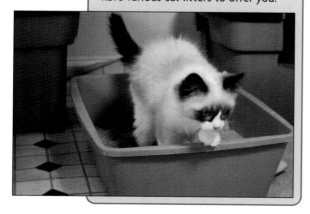

vertical surfaces. Some prefer public areas in which their human friends are present instead of secluded areas. It may be stress-related, as with scent marking, because scratching is another

territorial marker behaviour. In any case, the idea is to get your cat to scratch the post and not the carpets, furniture, drapes or the duvet on your bed.

Introduce your cat to the post by rubbing its paws on the post, hoping it will take the hint. Oftentimes the cat voluntarily attacks the post. Unfortunately, oftentimes it doesn't. If you catch your cat scratching in a forbidden area, startle it with a loud shout, banging a folded newspaper against your hand or something which will take its attention away from scratching. Never hit the cat. This will only get a revengeful reaction that might be dangerous.

RUBBISH RUMMAGING

Cats are inquisitive and may decide to have a good look through any interesting rubbish bins that are exuding an enticing odour. Normally, the answer is to remove the bin. However, if the attraction always seems to be kitchen rubbish, there may be a nutritional problem. Your cat may be searching for food because it is being underfed! It may alternatively be receiving an unbalanced diet and is trying to satisfy its inner need for a given missing ingredient.

Another possibility, and one which may be more appropriate to the indoors-only cat, is boredom or loneliness. These conditions can only be remedied by greater

Ragdolls and most other cats require something upon which they can scratch. This urge to scratch is both psychological and physical. You should introduce your Ragdoll to its scratching post immediately upon its arrival at your home.

interaction between owner and cat and/or obtaining a companion feline.

Clearly the cause should be identified. The immediate solution is to place the rubbish in a cupboard or similar place that is out of the cat's reach. This type of solution is called removal of the re-enforcer. It is a common method of overcoming problems across a number of unwanted behaviours. However, it does not correct the underlying problem that must still be addressed.

The first-time cat owner should not think that the problems discussed will likely be encountered. They are only met when the cat's environment is lacking in some way. Always remember that the older cat may have problems with bowel control. An extra litter tray at another location in the home will usually remedy this situation. Finally, if a problem is found and you are not able to remedy it, do seek the advice of your vet or breeder.

While the idea of becoming a breeder may appeal to many owners, the reality is more difficult than is often appreciated. It requires dedication, considerable investment of time and money, and the ability to cope with many heart-wrenching decisions and failures.

NEWBORN KITTENS

Most kittens are born with body hair. Their ears and eyes, however, remain closed for about two weeks, though some ears and eyes become functional after 72 hours. Kittens should be allowed to nurse for seven weeks, longer if they will not readily eat and drink from a plate. If allowed to nurse, most kittens will stay on their mother's milk for two months or more.

It would be quite impossible to discuss the complexities of practical breeding in only one chapter, so we will consider the important requirements of being a breeder plus basic feline reproductive information. This will enable you to better determine if, indeed, this aspect of the hobby is for you.

BEING A BREEDER

Apart from great affection for the breed, a successful breeding programme requires quantifiable objectives. Foremost among these is the rearing of healthy kittens free from known diseases. Next is the desire to produce offspring that are as good as, indeed better than, their parents.

Such objectives ensure that a breeder will endeavour to maintain standards and reduce or remove from the breed population any instances of dangerous diseases and conditions. Only stock registered and tested free of major diseases should ever be used. Adopting such a policy helps to counteract those who breed from inferior and often unhealthy cats.

To be a successful breeder you will need to become involved in the competition side of the hobby. Only via this route will you be able to determine if your programme is successful or not. Always remember that even the top-winning breeders still produce quite a high percentage of kittens that will only be of pet quality. There will be many disappointments along the road to even modest success.

THE DISADVANTAGES OF BREEDING

There are many rewards to be gained from breeding but the disadvantages should also be carefully considered. Kittens are demanding, especially once they are over three weeks of age. Rearing, vaccination, registration and veterinary bills will be costly. Any thoughts of profit should be dispelled. Homes must be found for the kittens, which will entail receiving many telephone calls—some at very inconvenient hours.

Many potential buyers will prove to be either unsuitable or 'time wasters' looking for the cheapest pedigreed cat obtainable. Kittens may die, while cats of any age could test positive for a major disease.

TOO MANY CATS

There are already too many cats in the world. In many countries, thousands of pathetic-looking felines can be seen wandering the streets in a badly emaciated state. They live tormented lives and have become a major social problem in many areas. There can be no excuse for these feral populations in developed Western nations. Quite frankly, some people who own cats, including some pedigreed owners, lack a sense of responsibility.

Cats allowed to roam in a non-neutered state are by far the main reason for the overpopulation problem. Unless a cat is of show or breeding quality, there is not a single justification for it to be bred or to remain in a non-neutered state. If your cat was purchased as a pet, you should help to resolve this global problem by having it neutered at the earliest possible date. This will make it a far healthier, happier and less problematic pet.

TOM FOOLERY

A non-neutered male cat kept as a single pet has little or no value for breeding purposes. It must be exhibited so it can gain some fame. The owner must have modern facilities to house both males and females. Females are always serviced at the home of the stud owner. This is extra responsibility and cost.

Such a male cannot be given any freedom to roam. If the tom is kept indoors, its scent-marking odours will often become intolerable. Even kept outdoors in a suitable cat pen, it will spray regularly to attract the attention of any females in the area. Toms are more assertive and often more aggressive than neutered males.

If they are allowed any outdoor freedom, they will become involved in battles with the local toms. Consequently, they will soon lose their handsome looks! Most cat breeders do not even keep entire males because of the problems and costs they entail. These cats are best kept in catteries where the owners have the time, the funds and everything else needed to justify their retention.

They may have to be put to sleep or given to a caring person who understands the problem.

Owning a number of cats will mean investing in cat pens. When females come into heat, they will try to escape and mate with any local tom with a twinkle in his eye! Their scent and calls will attract roving Romeos who will gather near your home and involve themselves in a series of raucous battles. Holidays and matings will need to be planned around hoped-for litter dates. All in all, owning only one or two breeding females is a major commitment.

Before deciding whether breeding really is something you want to do, what would make good sense would be to neuter the pet and then become an exhibitor. When you have exhibited a number of times, your knowledge of cats will be greater, as will your contacts.

CAT CALLS

Females left in a non-spayed state are far more at risk from diseases and infections of the uterus. When in heat, the female becomes unusually affectionate and provocative. Her calls, a sound once heard never forgotten, can become extremely annoying if she is left unmated.

WHAT'S A PEDIGREE WORTH?

When choosing breeding stock, never be dazzled by a pedigree. No matter how illustrious this is, it is only ever as good as the cat that bears it. If the cat is mediocre, then its prestigious pedigree is worthless from a breeding perspective. There are many other pitfalls for the novice when judging the value of a breeding line. These you must research in larger, more specialised books.

You will be more aware of what quality is all about and what it will cost for a well-bred female. It will be like an apprenticeship. Whether you then become a breeder, remain an exhibitor or prefer life as a pet owner, you will be glad you heeded the words of advice given here.

STOCK SELECTION

Stock selection revolves around health, quality, sex and age. Before these are discussed, it should be stated that many beginners unwisely rush this process. It is essential that ample time be devoted to researching from whom to purchase. This decision will influence a novice breeder's entire future endeavours.

HEALTH

Cats should only be obtained from a breeder whose stock has been tested negative for FeLV,

CAVEAT EMPTOR

When purchasing a kitten for breeding, make certain the seller knows what your intentions are. If a kitten is registered on the non-active register, this means it was not considered by its breeder to be good enough for breeding. Any kittens bred from such a cat cannot be registered. You should also check that the mother of the kitten/young adult you are interested in has tested negative for feline leukaemia and that all other vaccinations are current.

THE BREEDING QUEEN

A female used for breeding purposes is called a queen. The principal requirement of such a cat is that she is an excellent example of the breed. This does not mean she must be a show winner. Many a winning exhibition cat has proved to have little breeding value. This is because a show cat gains success purely on its appearance; however, it may not pass those looks to its offspring.

A good breeding female may lack that extra something needed to be a top winner. Yet, she may pass on most of her excellent features to her offspring. Much will depend on the breeding line from which she was produced. Therefore any potential breeder must research existing breeders to ascertain which have good track records of producing consistently high-quality cats. In truth, and sadly, few newcomers in their haste to become breeders make this extra effort. This can result in becoming disillusioned if the female produces only average to inferior kittens.

FIP and FIV. The stock should be current on all vaccinations and worm treatments. Additionally, its blood type should be known so as to avoid incompatibility problems.

QUALITY

This must come in two forms. One is in the individual cat's appearance; the other is in its genetic ability to pass on the quality of its parents. The best way of obtaining these paired needs is to obtain initial stock from a breeder having a proven record of success in Ragdolls, and with the colour you plan to start with. Being well acquainted with the breed's standard will be advantageous when seeking foundation stock. A female show cat attains her titles based on her appearance, but she may not pass on those looks to her offspring. Another cat that is very sound may pass on most of her good points and thus be more valuable for breeding. Of course, all litters will be influenced by the quality of the tom used. He will account for 50% of the offspring's genes. When viewing a litter of kittens, never forget that they are the result of the genes of two cats.

SEX

The beginner should only obtain females. The best advice is to commence with just one very sound female. By the time you have exhibited her and gained more knowledge about the finer points of the breed, you will be better able to judge what true quality is all about. By then you will also have made many contacts on the show circuit. Alternatively, you may decide breeding is not for you and will have invested the minimum of time and money. A male is not needed until a breeder has become established. Even then, owning one is not essential to success. There is no shortage of quality studs. Males create many problems the novice can do without. Once experience is gained is the time to decide if owning a male would be of any particular benefit.

AGE

There is no specific age at which stock should be purchased but the following are suggested.

1. Most people purchase young kittens so they can enjoy them. However, with such

THE MALE STUD

The selection of a suitable stud should have been planned months before, as it can take some time to find the best male to use. It is preferred that the breeding lines of the stud are compatible with those of the female, meaning both pedigrees will carry a number of the same individuals in them. This is termed line-breeding. The ideal male will excel in those features that are considered weak in the female. You may read in other books that if a female is weak in a given feature, the ideal stud will be the total opposite. However, this can be misleading.

If the female has an overly long tail, what you do not need is a stud with a short tail. Rather, his tail should be as near the ideal length as possible. Genetically, this will improve tail length in your line without introducing unwanted genetic variance in your stock. Compensatory matings, such as short tail to long tail, will create such variance. Once a male has been selected, ensure all his papers and vaccinations are in order. The female will be taken to the stud and left with him for a few days.

ROAMING ROMEOS

Males cats, toms, have extended testicles very early in life. By about nine months of age, the tom is capable of mating with a queen. Both queens and toms are polygamous and it is not uncommon for a queen to have a litter containing kittens fathered by different toms.

Quality comes in two forms: appearance and the genetic ability to pass on quality genes to offspring.

youngsters, their ultimate quality is harder to assess.

2. Chances are improved if a kitten has already won awards in shows. This will be when she is 14 weeks to 9 months of age, but she will be more costly.

3. A quality young female that has already produced offspring is a prudent choice but will be the most expensive option.

THE BREEDING PROCESS

Sexual maturity in cats may come as early as four months of age. Breeding should not be considered until the female is at least 12 months old, especially in the slow-maturing breeds. A young cat barely out of her kitten stage may not have the required physical or psychological stability to produce and raise a vigorous litter. After her first heat, a female will normally come into heat again every two to three weeks and continue to do so until mated. The actual oestrus period lasts three to eight days. It is during this time that she is receptive to a male.

Once the mating has been successful, the time between fertilisation and birth of the young, known as the gestation period, is in the range of 59 to 67 days, 63 or 64 days being typical. The litter size will generally be two to five. Kittens are born blind and helpless, but develop rapidly. Their eyes open about the seventh day. By 21 days they start exploring. At this time they will also be sampling solid foods. By eight weeks they can be vaccinated and neutered if required. Weaning normally commences by the age of six weeks and is completed within two to three weeks. Kittens can go to new homes when 12 weeks old, though 14 to 16 weeks is preferred. During this period you must decide if you wish to register the kittens or merely 'declare' them. This allows

THE HEAT IS ON

Most female cats reach sexual maturity by the time they are 28 weeks old. Females normally accept males from late winter to early fall, about a six-month period. They have a reproductive cycle of about two weeks and are in heat for about one of the two weeks. Intercourse causes the female to ovulate and pregnancy may last for about 66 days, perhaps longer in cold climates and shorter in the tropics.

Born helpless and blind, Ragdoll kittens require the constant attention of their mother as well as periodic supervision from the breeder.

them to be registered at a later time. Obtain the necessary information and forms from your cat-registration authority. You should also consider the benefits of registering your own breeder prefix. This, however, is only worthwhile if you intend to breed on a more than casual basis. If you have decided that certain kittens are unsuitable for showing/breeding, do consider early neutering.

Exhibiting Your
RAGDOLL CAT

ON THE CONTINENT AND BEYOND...

In Britain the title of UK Grand Champion or Premier is won in competition with other Grand titleholders. In mainland Europe cats can become International Champions. More British cats are expected to become International Champions with the recent introduction of passports for cats, allowing cats to compete more freely on the Continent and beyond. In countries other than Britain, the way in which shows are organised and titles achieved do differ somewhat. However, they broadly follow the outline discussed here.

Without shows, the cat fancy could not exist. There would be only a handful of breeds as compared with today's ever-growing list. There would be fewer colour patterns and far less cat awareness. Given the great importance of shows to the cat fancy, it is perhaps a little surprising, and disappointing, that the majority of cat owners have never visited a feline exhibition.

Shows such as the National and the Supreme of Britain, or their equivalents in other countries, are the shop windows of the world of domestic cats. They are meeting places where breeders from all over the country compete to establish how well their breeding programmes are developing. A show is also a major social event on the cat calendar.

Whether a potential pet owner or breeder of the future, you should visit one or two shows. It is a great day out for the whole family. Apart from the wonderful selection of breeds, there are also many trade stands. If a product is available, it will be seen at the large exhibitions.

Many of the national clubs and magazines have stands. The two major shows mentioned are held in the winter months, usually November and December. However, there are hundreds of other shows staged during the year in various parts of the country. They range from small local club events to major championship breed shows and are usually advertised in the cat magazines. Your ruling cat association can also supply a list of shows.

SHOW ORGANISATION

So you will have some idea of how things are organised, the following information will be helpful. You will learn even more by purchasing the show catalogue. This contains the names and addresses of the exhibitors and details of their cats. It also lists the prizes, indicates the show regulations, and carries many interesting advertisements.

A major show revolves around three broad categories of cats:
1. Unaltered cats, meaning those that are capable of breeding.
2. Neuters.
3. Non-pedigreed cats.

There is thus the opportunity for every type of cat, from the best of Ragdolls to the everyday 'moggie' pets, to take part. These three broad categories are divided into various sections. For example, the unaltered and

CLASSES AT SHOWS

Open	Any cat of the specified breed.
Novice	Cats that have never won a first prize.
Limit	Cats that have not won more than first prizes.
Junior	Cats over nine months of age but less than two years on the day of the show.
Senior	Cats over two years old.
Visitors	Cats living a given distance away from the show venue.
Assessment	Experimental breeds, which have an approved standard.
Aristocrat	Cats with one or two Challenge Certificates (or Premiers for neuters) so are not yet full Champions/Premiers.

neuters are divided into their respective sections, such as Longhair, Semi-Longhair, British, Foreign, Siamese and so on.

There are many more classes

Show cats must
be accustomed
to handling,
willing to accept
the judge's
inspection
without
resistance or
fright.

other than those mentioned. These
include club classes and those for
kittens and non-pedigreed cats.

JUDGING

There are two ways cats can be
judged. One is pen judging, the
other is bench or ring judging. In
Britain pen judging is the normal
method, though bench judging is
used for Best in Show. In pen

judging, the judge moves around
the cat pens. The cat gaining the
most points when compared to
the standard wins. In bench
judging, stewards take the cats to
the judge.

If a cat wins its class, it then
competes against other class
winners. By this process of
elimination, a cat may go on to
win the Best of Breed award. It

then competes against other breed winners for the Best in Group award. The group winners compete for the Best in Show award.

A breeder can gather a number of awards during the course of a show. Even those who do not own the very best cats can take pride in gaining second, third, fourth and recommended, especially if won at the larger shows. By progression, the top cat at a show will win its class, its breed, its section, and ultimately become the Best in Show exhibit. The titles a cat can win commence with that of Champion or Premier in the case of neuters. A Grand Champion is made after winning in competition with others of its same status. The same applies to a Grand Premier. The judging system may vary from one country to another but the basis remains as outlined.

THE SHOW CAT

When a cat is seen preening in its pen, the hard work that has gone into its preparation is rarely appreciated. Exhibits must be in peak condition and their coats in full bloom. The potential exhibit must gradually be trained to spend hours within its show pen. It must display no fear or aggression towards strangers, such as the stewards or the judges. These must be able to physically examine it, including its ears and

CLASSES FOR NON-PEDIGREED CATS

For non-pedigreed cats there are many classes, which include those for single colours, bicolours, tabbies, half-pedigreed, and so on. In this section are many delightful classes, such as those for cats owned by senior citizens, by young children (by age group), best original stray or rescued cat, best personality, most unusual looking, most photogenic, and best older cats. Within this cat section can be seen some truly gorgeous felines. There is no doubt that the pet classes have been the springboard that has launched many a top breeder into the world of pedigreed cats.

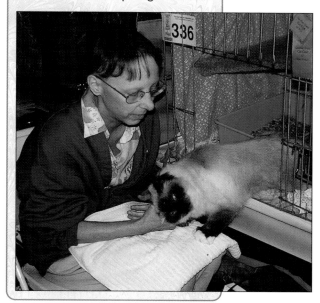

teeth; it also involves being lifted into the air. If a cat scratches or bites a judge, or any other show official, it is automatically withdrawn from the show. A repeat of this in the future would result, in most instances, in the cat's show career being terminated by the ruling association.

Apart from being comfortable with people peering into its pen, the cat must be able to endure

Much preparation and hard work goes into breeding and exhibiting a winning cat.

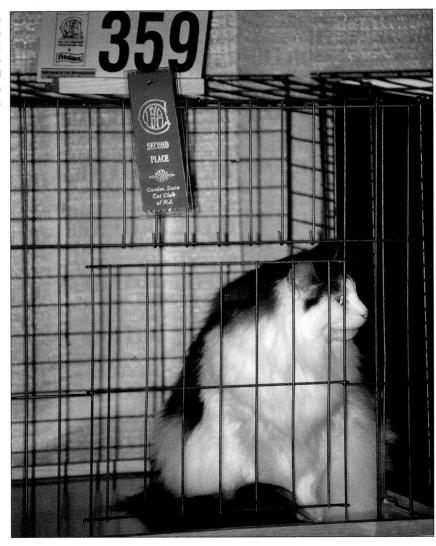

BECOMING AN EXHIBITOR

Before any hobbyist enters a show, he is advised to join a local cat club. Here, hobbyists will meet local breeders who will not only assess their cat for them but also provide help on many other topics. The novice exhibitor could attend one or two shows with an exhibitor in order to learn the ropes. During this period, he can become familiar with the show rules and regulations. These are quite extensive, intended to safeguard the best interests of the hobby, the exhibitors and, most importantly, the cats.

It is of interest to note that some breeders own cats in partnership with other fanciers. This is useful when one person enjoys the breeding and the other the exhibition side. It enables both to really be involved in the hobby to a level that might not have been possible for either on his own. So, whether you fancy being an exhibitor or just love cats, do make a point of visiting the next major show in your area. You may just find the experience addictive!

long journeys to the show venue. Unless trained the cat may become a nervous, aggressive feline that will have a very short show career.

Obviously the cat must display quality. This means having none of the major faults that would prevent it from gaining a first prize. These are listed in the breed standard. The meaning of quality is very subjective. You do not need to own a potential champion to be a successful exhibitor. The cat must also be registered with the association under whose rules the show is being run. In Britain this will be the GCCF or The Cat Association of Britain.

As in anything competitive, exhibits can gain prizes at the lower levels of a hobby without having any realistic chance of awards in the major shows. Owning such exhibits is often part of a top breeder/exhibitor's portfolio from their early days in the hobby. Others may never move beyond the smaller shows but still gain reputations for owning sound stock. They thoroughly enjoy being involved at their given level.

If the idea of exhibiting appeals to you, the best way to make a start is to join a local club. There you not only will be advised on all procedures but also will be able to make many new friends. Exhibiting can be costly in cash and time, but you can focus on the more local shows while attending the larger ones as a visitor.

Maintaining a cat in the peak of good health revolves around the implementation of a sound husbandry strategy. At the basic level, this means being responsible about feeding, cleanliness and grooming. However, in spite of an owner's best efforts in these matters, cats may still become ill due to other causes. Although owners can attempt to prevent, identify and react to problems, only a vet is qualified to diagnose and suggest and/or effect remedies. Attempts by owners or 'informed' friends to diagnose and treat for specific diseases are dangerous and potentially life-threatening to the cat.

A DELICATE HEART

A cat's heart is as delicate as a human's heart, but it is much smaller. At full maturity, queens' hearts weigh between 9-12 grammes. Toms' hearts are heavier, weighing 11-18 grammes. The blood that circulates through the heart chambers does not supply the heart muscle, which requires a separate circulatory system.

SELECTING A VETERINARY SURGEON

Your selection of a veterinary surgeon should not be based upon personality (as most are) but upon convenience to your home. You want a vet who is close because you might have emergencies or need to make multiple visits for treatments. You want a vet who

Veterinary surgeons are usually equipped with modern diagnostic equipment to ascertain the health and condition of your Ragdoll.

has services that you might require such as nail clipping and bathing, as well as sophisticated pet supplies and a good reputation for ability and responsiveness. There is nothing more frustrating than having to wait a day or more to get a response from your veterinary surgeon.

All veterinary surgeons are licensed and their diplomas and/or certificates should be displayed in their waiting rooms. There are, however, many veterinary specialities that usually require further studies and internships. There are specialists in heart problems (veterinary cardiologists), skin problems (veterinary dermatologists), teeth and gum problems (veterinary dentists), eye problems (veterinary ophthalmologists) and x-rays (veterinary radiologists), as well as vets who have specialities in reproduction, nutrition and behaviour. Most veterinary surgeons do routine surgery, such as neutering and stitching up wounds. When the problem affecting your cat is serious, it is not unusual or impudent to get another medical opinion, although in Britain you are obliged to advise the vets concerned about this. You might also want to compare costs among several veterinary surgeons. Sophisticated health care and veterinary services can be very costly. It is not infrequent that important decisions are based upon financial considerations.

BLOOD GROUP INCOMPATIBILITY (BGI)

In recent years, blood group incompatibility has become the focus of scientists, vets and breeders. Its importance to pet owners is when transfusions are needed. For breeders it probably accounts for a large percentage of kittens that die from fading kitten syndrome. Scientifically the problem is called neonatal erythrolysis, meaning the destruction of red blood cells in newly born offspring.

Cats have two blood groups, A & B. Group A is dominant to B (which is genetically called recessive). When the antibodies of B group mothers are passed to A group kittens, via her colostrum milk, they destroy red blood cells. Death normally follows within a few days.

Most domestic cats tested are group A. However, national and regional differences display a variation in which 1-6% may be of type B. In pedigreed breeds it has been found that the number of group B cats varies significantly. The following breeds, based on present available data, have the indicated percentage incidence of group B blood type.

0%	Siamese, Burmese and Oriental Shorthair
1-5%	Maine Coon, Manx and Norwegian Forest
10-20%	Abyssinian, Birman, Japanese Bobtail, Persian, Scottish Fold and Somali
25-50%	British Shorthair, Devon and Cornish Rex and Exotic Shorthair

The clear implication to breeders is to establish their cats' blood group, via testing, and conduct appropriate matings. These should not result in B group mothers nursing A group kittens. The safe matings are:

1. Group A males   x   A females
2. Group B males   x   A or B females
3. Group A females   x   A or B males
4. Group B females   x   B males

Breeders are advised to seek further information before embarking on stock purchase and breeding programmes.

PREVENTATIVE MEDICINE

It is much easier, less costly and more effective to practise preventative medicine than to fight bouts of illness and disease. Properly bred kittens come from parents who were selected based upon their genetic disease profile. Their mothers should have been vaccinated, free of all internal and external parasites and properly nourished. For these reasons, a visit to the veterinary surgeon who cared for the queen is recommended. The queen can pass on disease resistance to her kittens, which can last for eight to ten weeks. She can also pass on parasites and many infections. That's why

CARE OF FELINE KIDNEYS

The kidney of the cat is larger than that of the dog, but it has the typical bean shape. It receives 25% of the blood output of the heart! For this reason it has rather significant veins to accommodate this large supply of blood, and injuries suffered by the kidneys are usually serious and may be frequent.

you should visit the veterinary surgeon who cared for the queen.

VACCINATIONS

Most vaccinations are given by injection and should only be done by a veterinary surgeon. Both he and you should keep a record of

HEALTH AND VACCINATION SCHEDULE

Age	6 WKS	8 WKS	10 WKS	12 WKS	16 WKS	6 MOS	1 YR
Worm Control	✔	✔	✔		✔		
Neutering						✔	
Rhinotracheitis	✔	✔		✔	✔		✔
Panleukopenia	✔	✔		✔			✔
Calicivirus		✔			✔		✔
Feline Leukaemia				✔			✔
Feline Infectious Peritonitis				✔	✔		✔
Faecal Evaluation						✔	
Feline Immunodeficiency Testing							✔
Feline Leukaemia Testing				✔			✔
Dental Evaluation		✔				✔	
Rabies*				✔	✔		✔

Vaccinations are not instantly effective. It takes about two weeks for the cat's immune system to develop antibodies. Most vaccinations require annual booster shots. Your veterinary surgeon should guide you in this regard.
* Not seen in the UK.

DISEASE REFERENCE CHART

	What is it?	Cause	Symptoms
Feline Leukaemia Virus (FeLV)	Infectious disease; kills more cats each year than any other feline infectious disease.	A virus spread through saliva, tears, urine and faeces of infected cats; bite wounds.	Early on no symptoms may occur, but eventually infected cats experience signs from depression and weight loss to respiratory distress. FeLV also suppresses immune system, making a cat susceptible to almost any severe chronic illness.
Rabies	Potentially deadly virus that infects warm-blooded mammals. Not seen in the United Kingdom.	A bacterium, often carried by rodents, that enters through mucous membranes and spreads quickly throughout the body.	Aggressiveness, a blank or vacant look in the eyes, increased vocalisation and/or weak or wobbly gait.
Feline Infectious Enteritis (FIE) *aka Panleukopenia*	Highly contagious virus, potentially deadly.	Ingestion of the virus, which is usually spread through the faeces of infected cats.	Most common: severe diarrhoea. Also vomiting, fatigue, lack of appetite, severe inflammation of intestines.
Feline Viral Rhinotracheitis (FVR)	Viral disease that affects eyes and upper respiratory tracts.	A virus that can affect any cat, especially those in multiple-cat settings.	Sneezing attacks, coughing, drooling thick saliva, fever, watery eyes, ulcers of mouth, nose and eyes.
Feline Immuno-deficiency Virus (FIV)	Virus that reduces white blood cells.	An infection spread commonly through cat-fight wounds.	Signs may be dormant for years or innocuous, such as diarrhoea or anaemia.
Feline Infectious Peritonitis (FIP)	A fatal viral disease, may be linked to FeLV and FIV.	Bacteria in dirty litter boxes; stress may increase susceptibility in kittens.	Extremely variable; range from abdominal swelling to chest problems, eye ailments and body lesions.
Feline Urological Syndrome (FUS)	A disease that affects the urinary tract of cats.	Inflammation of bladder and urethra.	Constipation, constant licking of penis or vulva, blood in urine (males), swollen abdomen, crying when lifted.

the date of the injection, the identification of the vaccine and the amount given. The first vaccination is normally given when the kitten is about 8–9 weeks old. About 30 days later a booster is given. Although there are many diseases to which a cat may fall victim, the most dangerous three—FIE, FVR and FeLV—can be safeguarded against with a single (three-in-one) injection. Thereafter an annual booster is all that is required.

MAJOR DISEASES
There are a number of diseases for which there is either no cure or little chance of recovery. However, some can be prevented by vaccination. All breeders and owners should ensure kittens are so protected.

FELINE INFECTIOUS ENTERITIS (FIE)
This is also known as feline panleukopenia, feline distemper and feline parvovirus. The virus attacks the intestinal system. It is

THE RIB CAGE

Cats usually have 13 pairs of ribs. The ribs in the middle are longer than the ribs on either end (or beginning) of the rib cage. The first nine ribs are joined to the chest bone (sternum) with costal cartilages. Ribs 10, 11 and 12 are also associated with cartilage, which contributes to the costal arch. The thirteenth rib is called the floating rib and its cartilage is separate from the other ribs.

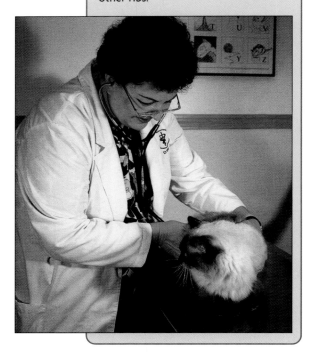

spread via the faeces and urine. The virus may survive for many years in some environments. The use of household bleach (sodium hypochlorite) for cleaning helps

to prevent colonisation. Signs, among others, are diarrhoea, vomiting, depression, anorexia and dehydration. Death may occur within days. A vaccine is available.

FELINE VIRAL RHINOTRACHEITIS (FVR) & CALICIVIRUS (FCV)

Also known as cat flu, this is a complex of upper respiratory diseases. Signs are excessive hard sneezing, runny nose and mouth ulcers. Cats vaccinated after having contracted flu may recover but may suffer recurrent bouts, especially if they become stressed.

FELINE LEUKAEMIA VIRUS (FeLV)

This is a highly infectious viral disease. It is spread via direct contact—mutual grooming, saliva, feeding bowls, faeces, urine and biting. It can be passed prenatally from a female to her offspring. It creates tumours, anaemia, immune system depression, pyrexia (high temperatures), lethargy, respiratory disease, intestinal disease and many other potentially fatal problems. It is most prevalent in high-density cat populations. Not all cats will be affected, but they may become carriers.

Kittens less than six months old are especially vulnerable. Infected cats usually die by the time they are three to four years old. Cats can be screened or tested for this disease. Vaccination is not

100% effective but is recommended in kittens being sold into multi-cat environments.

FELINE IMMUNODEFICIENCY VIRUS (FIV)

This causes the white blood cells to be significantly reduced, thus greatly suppressing the efficiency of the immune system. It is not transferable to humans. Infection is normally gained from cat-fight wounds; thus, outdoor males are at the most risk. A cat diagnosed via blood tests as FIV-positive may live a normal life for months or years if retained indoors and given careful attention. Signs may be innocuous in the early stages, such as anaemia or diarrhoea. No vaccine is available.

FELINE INFECTIOUS PERITONITIS (FIP)

This viral disease is invariably fatal once contracted in its more potent forms. However, the virulence of the virus is variable and may by destroyed by the immune system. Stress may increase susceptibility in kittens. It may be linked to FeLV and FIV. Signs are extremely variable and range from abdominal swelling to chest problems, eye ailments to body lesions. There are various tests available but none is as yet 100% conclusive. Strict cleanliness is essential, especially of litter trays. No vaccine is available.

FELINE UROLOGICAL SYNDROME (FUS)

This is a very distressing condition caused by an inflammation of the bladder and urethra. Signs are constipation-like squatting and attempts to urinate, regular licking of the penis or vulva, blood in urine (males), swollen abdomen, crying when lifted and urinating in unusual places (often with only small amounts).

The numerous causes include: infection, dirty litter tray of the indoor cat, alkaline urine (in cats it should be acidic), diet too dry, lack of water intake (even though this may be available) and being hit by a vehicle (damaged nerves). Veterinary treatment is essential or the condition could be fatal due to the bladder bursting or the presence of dangerous bacteria.

RABIES

Britain and most European Community countries are free of this terrible disease. The stringent quarantine laws of Britain are such that vaccination is not necessary. However, the introduction of passports for dogs and cats means that resident British cats must be vaccinated if they are to travel abroad and return to the UK without being placed into quarantine. The vaccination is given when the kitten is three or more months old. The pet passport process

KEEPING YOUR CAT HEALTHY

Although there are a multitude of ailments, diseases and accidents that could befall a cat, all but the most minor of problems can be avoided with good management. The following tips are a recipe for keeping your cat in the best of health.

- Make sure it is vaccinated and in other ways protected from each of the major diseases. It must also receive annual boosters to maintain immunity.
- Have periodic checks made by your vet to see if your cat has worms.
- Ensure the cat receives an adequate diet that is both appealing and balanced.
- Have the kitten neutered if it is not to be used for breeding.
- Ensure the cat's litter tray, food/water vessels and grooming tools are always maintained in spotless condition.
- Do not let your cat out overnight or when you are away working or shopping.
- Always wash your hands after gardening or petting other people's pets.
- Groom your cat daily. If this is done, you will more readily notice fleas or other problems than if grooming was done less frequently.
- Never try to diagnose and treat problems that are clearly of an internal type. Remember, even the most informed of breeders is not a vet and unable to reliably diagnose problems for you or advise treatments. Contact your vet.
- If you are ever in doubt about the health of your cat, do not delay in discussing your concerns with your vet. Delays merely allow problems to become more established.

takes at least six months to complete, so plan well ahead.

COMMON HEALTH PROBLEMS

DERMATITIS (ECZEMA)

Dry, lifeless coat, loss of coat, tiny scabs over the head and body, loose flakes (dandruff) and excessive scratching are all commonly called eczema. The cause covers a range of possibilities including diet, parasitic mites such as *Cheyletiella spp.*, fungus or an allergy to flea or other bites. Sometimes reasons are unknown. Veterinary diagnosis and treatment are required.

RINGWORM (DERMATOPHYTOSIS)

This problem is fungal, not that of a worm. The most common form is *Microsporum canis*, which accounts for over 90% of cases. Cats less than one year old are at the highest risk, while longhaired breeds are more prone to the problem than shorthaired cats. The fungi feed on the keratin layers of the skin, nails and hair. Direct contact and spores that remain in the environment are the main means of transmission.

Typical signs are circular-type bald areas of skin, which may be flaked and reddish. The coat generally may become dry and lifeless, giving the appearance of numerous other skin and hair problems. Veterinary diagnosis

There is skill involved to opening a cat's mouth. Don't try it without having your vet show you the proper way to do it.

POSSIBLE SOURCES OF EAR PROBLEMS

- Fight scratches
- Excess secretion of wax
- Swellings and blood blisters (haematoma) resulting from intrusion by foreign bodies (grass, etc.)
- Sunburn
- Whitish-coloured ear mites (*Otodectes cynotis*)
- Orange-coloured harvest mites (*Trombicula autumnalis*)
- Fleas
- Bacterial infection of either the outer or middle/inner ear

and treatment, either topical or via drugs, is essential as the condition is zoonotic, meaning it can be transferred to humans.

EAR PROBLEMS

Most of the common ear problems affect the outer ear. The telltale sign is the cat's constant scratching of the ears and/or its holding the ear to one side. Greasy hairs around the ear, dark brown wax (cerumen) in the ears, scaly flakes in or around the ear or minute white or orange pinhead-like bodies (mites) in the ear are common signs. Canker is a term used for ear infections, but it has no specific meaning.

Over-the-counter remedies for ear problems are ineffective unless correct diagnosis has been made. It is therefore better to let the vet diagnose and treat the cat. Some problems may require anaesthesia and minor surgery.

DIARRHOEA

This is a general term used to indicate a semi-liquid to liquid state of faecal matter. Mild to acute cases may be due to a change of environment, dietary change, eating an 'off' item, gorging on a favoured food, stress or a minor chill. These often rectify themselves within days. Chronic and persistent diarrhoea may be the result of specific diseases. Any indication of blood in the faecal matter must be considered dangerous.

In minor cases, withholding food for 12–24 hours, or feeding a simple diet, may arrest the condition. If not, contact your vet. Faecal analysis and blood testing may be required. By answering numerous questions related to the cat's diet, general health, level of activity, loss of appetite, etc., the vet will determine whether tests are required or if immediate treatment is warranted. Do not

Most veterinary surgeons request or require the presence and assistance of the cat's owner during routine examinations.

give cats human or canine
intestinal remedies; these could
prove dangerous.

CONSTIPATION

When a cat strains but is unable
to pass motions, this is indicative

NEUTERING

Neutering is a major means of avoiding
ill health. It dramatically reduces the risk
of males becoming involved in territorial
battles with the dangers of physical
injury and disease transference. It makes
the male more placid and less likely to
scent mark its home. It also reduces the
incidence of prostate problems, and
there is no risk of testicular cancer. The
female avoids potentially lethal illnesses
related to her being allowed to remain in
an unmated condition, such as breast
cancer.

Neutering is usually performed
between four and six months of age but
it can be done as early as eight weeks of
age. Data available on the age at which a
kitten is neutered indicate that early
neutering has more advantages than
drawbacks. Breeders should have this
performed on all cats sold as pets.

Male cats are neutered. The
operation removes the testicles and
requires that the cat be anaesthetised.
Females are spayed. This is major
surgery during which the ovaries and
uterus are removed. Both males and
females should be kept quiet at home
for about seven to ten days following
the procedure, at which time the vet
will remove the sutures.

of various causes. It may have
hairballs, may have eaten a bird or
rodent and has a bone lodged in

CLEANLINESS IS THE KEY

Crucial to the prevention and spread of disease is the need to maintain meticulous cleanliness, especially relating to the litter tray. Many diseases and problems are transferred via faecal matter. Once a problem is suspected, the advice of a vet should be sought. Blood tests, faecal microscopy and other testing methods are now available. They can mean the difference between life and death of a cherished pet.

its intestinal tract, may be suffering from a urological

problem rather than constipation, or may have been hit by a car and has damaged the nerves that control bowel movements. As constipation is potentially serious, veterinary advice should be sought. Laxatives and faecal softener tablets may be given, the faecal matter can be surgically removed or another treatment carried out.

STRESS TEST

Stress reduces the effectiveness of the immune system. Seemingly innocuous conditions may develop into major problems or leave the cat more open to attack by disease. Stress is difficult to identify specifically, but its major causes are well known. These include incorrect diet, intrusion by another cat in its home or territory, excessive handling and petting, disturbed sleep, uncomfortable home temperatures, bullying by another cat or pet, parasitic infestation, boarding in a cattery, travel, moving home, boredom, limited accommodation space and, for some felines, being exhibited.

A healthy Ragdoll
is a happy Ragdoll.

EXTERNAL PARASITES

FLEAS

Of all the problems to which cats are prone, none is more well known and frustrating than fleas. Indeed, flea-related problems are the principal cause of visits to veterinary surgeons. Flea infestation is relatively simple to cure but difficult to prevent. Periodic flea checks for your cat, conducted with annual health check-ups, are highly recommended. Consistent dosing with anthelmintic preparations is also advised. Parasites that are harboured inside the body are a bit more difficult to eradicate but they are easier to control.

To control a flea infestation you have to understand the flea's life cycle. Fleas are often thought of as a summertime problem but centrally heated homes have changed the life-cycle patterns, and fleas can be found at any time of the year. Fleas thrive in hot and humid environments; they soon die if the temperature drops below 35°F. The most effective method of flea control is a two-stage approach: one stage to kill the adult fleas, and the other to control the development of pre-adult fleas. Unfortunately, no

A male flea.

single active ingredient is effective against all stages of the life cycle.

LIFE CYCLE STAGES

During its life, a flea will pass through four life stages: egg, larva, pupa and adult. The adult stage is the most visible and irritating stage of the flea life cycle, and this is why the majority of flea-control products concentrates on this stage. The fact is that adult fleas account for only 1% of the total flea population, and the other 99% exist in pre-adult stages, i.e. eggs, larvae and pupae. The pre-adult stages are barely visible to the naked eye.

THE LIFE CYCLE OF THE FLEA

Eggs are laid on the cat, usually in quantities of about 20 or 30, several times a day. The female adult flea must have a blood meal before each egg-laying session. When first laid, the eggs will not cling to the cat's fur, as the eggs are not sticky. They will immediately fall to the floor or ground, especially if the cat moves around or scratches.

Once the eggs fall from the cat onto the carpet or furniture, they will hatch into yellow larvae, approximately 2 mms long. This takes from 5 to 11 days. Larvae are not particularly mobile, and

A Look at Fleas

Fleas have been around for millions of years and have adapted to changing host animals. They are able to go through a complete life cycle in less than one month or they can extend their lives to almost two years by remaining as pupae or cocoons. They must have a blood meal every 10-14 days, and egg production begins within two days of their first meal. The female cat flea is very prolific and can lay 2000 eggs in her lifetime!

Fleas have been measured as being able to jump 300,000 times and can jump 150 times their length in any direction, including straight up. Those are just a few of the reasons why they are so successful in infesting a cat!

A scanning electron micrograph (S. E. M.) of a flea.

S. E. M. BY DR DENNIS KUNKEL, UNIVERSITY OF HAWAII

Magnified head of a flea.

S. E. M. BY DR DENNIS KUNKEL, UNIVERSITY OF HAWAII

will usually travel only a few inches from where they hatch. However, they do have a tendency to move away from light and heavy traffic—under furniture, in the carpet and behind doors are common places to find high quantities of flea larvae.

The flea larvae feed on dead organic matter, including adult flea faeces, until they are ready to change into adult fleas. Fleas will usually remain as larvae for around seven days, becoming darker in colour. After this period, the larvae will pupate a protective cocoon. While inside the pupae, the larvae will undergo metamorphosis and change into adult fleas. This can happen within a week, but the adult fleas can remain inside the pupae waiting to hatch for up to six months. The pupae are signalled to hatch by certain stimuli, such as physical pressure—the pupae's being stepped on, heat from an animal lying on the pupae or increased carbon dioxide levels and vibrations—indicating that a suitable host is available.

DID YOU KNOW?
Never mix flea control products without first consulting your veterinary surgeon. Some products can become toxic when combined with others and can cause serious or fatal consequences.

DID YOU KNOW?
Flea-killers are poisonous. You should not spray these toxic chemicals on areas of a cat's body that he licks, on his genitals or on his face. Flea killers taken internally are a better answer, but check with your vet in case internal therapy is not advised for your cat.

Once hatched, the adult flea must feed within a few days. Once the adult flea finds a host, it will not leave voluntarily. It only becomes dislodged by grooming or the host animal's scratching. The adult flea will remain on the host for the duration of its life unless forcibly removed.

TREATING THE ENVIRONMENT AND THE CAT

Treating fleas should be a two-pronged attack. First, the environment needs to be treated; this includes carpets and furniture, especially the cat's bedding and areas underneath furniture. The environment should be treated with a household spray containing an Insect Growth Regulator (IGR) and an insecticide to kill the adult fleas. There are also liquids, given orally, that contain chitin inhibitors. These render flea eggs incapable of development. There are both foam and liquid wipe-on treatments. Additionally, cats can

Opposite page: A scanning electron micrograph of a flea, magnified more than 100x. This image has been colorized for effect.

The Life Cycle of the Flea

Eggs

Larva

Pupa

Photos courtesy of Fleabusters® Rx for Fleas.

Adult

Flea Control

IGR (INSECT GROWTH REGULATOR)

Two types of products should be used when treating fleas—a product to treat the pet and a product to treat the home. Adult fleas represent 1% of the flea population. The pre-adult fleas (eggs, larvae and pupae) represent 99% of the flea population and are found in the environment; it is in the case of pre-adult fleas that products containing an Insect Growth Regulator (IGR) should be used in the home.

IGRs are a new class of compounds used to prevent the development of insects. They do not kill the insect outright, but instead use the insect's biology against it to stop it from completing its growth. Products that contain methoprene are the world's first and leading IGRs. Used to control fleas and other insects, this type of IGR will stop flea larvae from developing and protect the house for up to seven months.

EN GARDE: CATCHING FLEAS OFF GUARD!

Consider the following ways to arm yourself against fleas:

• Add a small amount of pennyroyal or eucalyptus oil to your cat's bath. These natural remedies repel fleas.
• Supplement your cat's food with fresh garlic (minced or grated) and a hearty amount of brewer's yeast, both of which ward off fleas.
• Use a flea comb on your cat daily. Submerge fleas in a cup of bleach to kill them quickly.
• Confine the cat to only a few rooms to limit the spread of fleas in the home.
• Vacuum daily...and get all of the crevices! Dispose of the bag every few days until the problem is under control.
• Wash your cat's bedding daily. Cover cushions where your cat sleeps with towels, and wash the towels often.

be injected with treatments that can last up to six months. Emulsions that have the same effect can also be added to food. The advanced treatments are only available from veterinary surgeons. The IGRs actually mimic the fleas' own hormones and stop the eggs and larvae from developing into adult fleas. There are currently no treatments available to attack the pupa stage of the life cycle, so the adult insecticide is used to kill the newly hatched adult fleas before they find a host. Most IGRs are active for many months, while adult insecticides are only active for a few days.

When treating with a household spray, it is a good idea to vacuum before applying the product. This stimulates as many pupae as possible to hatch into adult fleas. The vacuum cleaner should also be treated with a flea treatment to prevent the eggs and larvae that have been hoovered into the vacuum bag from hatching.

The second stage of treatment is to apply an adult insecticide to the cat usually in the form of a collar or a spray. Alternatively, there are drops that, when placed on the back of the animal's neck, spread throughout the fur and skin to kill adult fleas. A word of warning: Never use products sold for dogs on your cat; the result could be fatal.

PHOTO BY DWIGHT R KUHN

Dwight R Kuhn's magnificent action photo, showing a flea jumping.

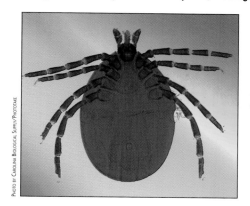

PHOTO BY CAROLINA BIOLOGICAL SUPPLY/PHOTOTAKE

A brown tick, *Rhipicephalus sanguineus*, is an uncommon but annoying tick found on cats.

PHOTO BY DR DENNIS KUNKEL, UNIVERSITY OF HAWAII

The head of a tick, *Dermacentor variabilis*, enlarged and coloured for effect.

TICKS AND MITES

Though not as common as fleas, ticks and mites are found all over the tropical and temperate world. They don't bite, like fleas; they harpoon. They dig their sharp proboscis (nose) into the cat's skin and drink the blood. Their only food and drink is cat's blood. Cats can get potentially fatal anaemia, paralysis and many other diseases from ticks and mites. They may live where fleas are found and they like to hide in cracks or seams in walls wherever cats live. They are controlled the same way fleas are controlled.

The *Dermacentor variabilis* may well be the most common tick in many geographical areas, especially those areas where the climate is hot and humid. The other common ticks that attack small animals are *Rhipicephalus sanguineus, Ixodes* and some species of *Amblyomma.*

Most ticks have life expectancies of a week to six months, depending upon climatic conditions. They can neither jump nor fly, but they can crawl slowly and can range up to 5 metres (16 feet) to reach a sleeping or unsuspecting animal.

INTERNAL PARASITES

Most animals—fishes, birds and mammals, including cats and humans—have worms and other parasites that live inside their bodies. According to Dr Herbert R Axelrod, the fish pathologist, there are two kinds of parasites: dumb and smart. The smart parasites live in peaceful cooperation with their hosts (symbiosis), while the dumb parasites kill their host. Most of the worm infections are relatively easy to control. If they are not controlled

---

TOXOPLASMOSIS AND PREGNANT WOMEN

Toxoplasmosis is caused by a single parasite, *Toxoplasma gondii*. Cats acquire it by eating infected prey, such as rodents or birds, or raw meat. Obviously, strictly indoor cats are at less risk of infection than cats that are permitted to roam outdoors. Symptoms include diarrhoea, listlessness, pneumonia and inflammation of the eye. Sometimes there are no symptoms. The disease can be treated with antibiotics.

The only way humans can get the disease is through direct contact with the cat's faeces. People usually don't display any symptoms, although they can show mild flu-like symptoms. Once exposed, an antibody is produced and the person builds immunity to the disease.

The real danger to humans is that pregnant women can pass the parasite to the developing foetus. In this case the chances are good that the baby will be born with a major health problem and/or serious birth defects. In order to eliminate risk, pregnant women should have someone else deal with the litter-box duties or wear gloves while taking care of the litter-box and wash hands thoroughly afterwards.

Opposite page: The tick, *Dermacentor variabilis*, is one of the most common ticks found on cats. Look at the strength in its eight legs! No wonder it's hard to detach them.

INTERNAL PARASITES OF CATS

NAME	DESCRIPTION	SYMPTOMS	ACQUISITION	TREATMENT
Roundworm (*Toxocara cati* and *Toxascaris leonina*)	Large white coil-like worms, 2–4 inches long, resembling small springs.	Vomiting, pot belly, respiratory problems, poor growth rate, protruding third eyelids, poor haircoat.	Ingesting infective larvae; ingesting infected mammals, birds or insects; a queen with *Toxocari cati* nursing kittens.	Anthelmintics; scrupulously clean environment (e.g. daily removal of all faeces recommended).
***Physaloptera* species**	1–6 inches long, attacks the wall of the stomach.	Vomiting, anorexia, melena.	Eating insects that live in soil (e.g. May beetles).	Diagnosed with a gastroscope; treated with pyrantel pamoate. Prevention of exposure to the intermediate hosts.
***Gordius* or Horsehair worm**	6-inch pale brown worms with stripes.	Vomiting.	May ingest a worm while drinking from or making contact with swimming pools and toilet bowls.	Anthelmintics; avoiding potentially infected environments.
Hookworm (*Ancylostoma tubaeforme*)	The adult worms, ranging from 6 to 15 mms in length, attach themselves to the small intestines.	Anaemia, melena, weight loss, poor haircoat.	Larva penetrating the cat's skin, usually attacks the small intestine. Found in soil and flower gardens where faecal matter is deposited.	Fortnightly treatment with anthelmintics. Good sanitation (e.g. daily cleanup of litter boxes).
Tapeworm (*Dipylidium caninum* and *Taenia taeniformis*)	Up to 3 feet long. Parts shaped similar to cucumber seeds. The most common intermediate hosts are fleas and biting lice.	No clinical signs—difficult to detect.	Eating infected adult fleas. Uses rodents as hosts.	Praziquantel and epsiprantel. Management of environment to ensure scrupulously clean conditions. Proper flea control.

they weaken the host cat to the point that other medical problems occur, but they are not dumb parasites.

HOOKWORMS

The worm *Ancylostoma tubaeforme* can inject a cat by larva penetrating its skin. It attaches itself to the small intestine of the cat, where it sucks blood. This loss of blood could cause iron-deficiency anaemia.

Outdoor cats that spend much of their time in the garden or in contact with soil are commonly injected with hookworm. There is another worm, the *Gordius* or horsehair worm, that, if ingested by cat, causes vomiting.

TAPEWORMS

There are many species of tapeworms. They are carried by

DEWORMING

Ridding your kitten of worms is VERY IMPORTANT because certain worms that kittens carry, such as tapeworms and roundworms, can infect humans.

Breeders initiate a deworming programme at or about four weeks of age. The routine is repeated every two or three weeks until the kitten is three months old. The breeder from whom you obtained your kitten should provide you with the complete details of the deworming programme.

Your veterinary surgeon can prescribe and monitor the programme of deworming for you. The usual programme is treating the kitten every 15–20 days until the kitten is positively worm-free.

It is advised that you only treat your kitten with drugs that are recommended professionally.

The head and rostellum (the round prominence on the scolex) of a tapeworm, which infects cats and humans.

fleas! The cat eats the flea and starts the tapeworm cycle. Humans can also be infected with tapeworms, so don't eat fleas! Fleas are so small that your cat could pass them onto your hands, your plate or your food and thus make it possible for you to ingest a flea that is carrying tapeworm eggs.

While tapeworm infection is not life-threatening in cats (smart parasite!), it can be the cause of a very serious liver disease for

Magnified heartworm larvae, *Dirofilaria immitis*.

PHOTO BY CAROLINA BIOLOGICAL SUPPLY/PHOTOTAKE

The heartworm, *Dirofilaria immitis*.

PHOTO BY JAMES E HAYDEN, RPB/PHOTOTAKE

humans. About 50 percent of the humans infected with *Echinococcus multilocularis*, a type of tapeworm that causes alveolar hydatis, perish.

HEARTWORMS

Heartworms are thin, extended worms up to 30 cms (12 ins) long, which are difficult to diagnose in cats as the worms are too few to be identified by the antigen-detection test. Symptoms may be loss of energy, loss of appetite, coughing, the development of a pot belly and anaemia. Heartworm injection in cats should be treated very seriously as it is often fatal.

Heartworms are transmitted by mosquitoes. The mosquito drinks the blood of an infected cat and takes in larvae with the blood. It takes two to three weeks for the larvae to develop to the infective stage within the body of the mosquito. Cats are less frequently injected with heartworms than dogs are. Also, the parasite is more likely to attack the cat's brain or other organs rather than the heart. Cats should be treated at about six weeks of age, and maintained on a prophylactic dose given monthly.

First Aid at a Glance

BURNS/SCALDS
Place the affected area under cool water; use ice if only a small area is burnt. Do not cover the burn or clip hair away. Petroleum jelly can be applied; take cat to vet immediately.

CHEMICAL BURNS
Wash with water only. If you know the chemical is acid, a weak solution of sodium bicarbonate will help, or a vinegar solution will do for alkaline burns.

BEE/INSECT BITES
Apply freshly sliced onion. Apply ice to relieve swelling; antihistamine dosed properly.

AUTOMOBILE ACCIDENT
Move cat from roadway with blanket; seek veterinary aid.

ANIMAL BITES
Clean any bleeding area; apply pressure until bleeding subsides; go to the vet.

SHOCK
Calm the cat, keep him warm and in a horizontal position; seek immediate veterinary aid.

SPIDER BITES
Use cold compress and a pressurised pack to inhibit venom's spreading.

NOSEBLEED
Apply cold compress to the nose; apply pressure to any visible abrasion.

ANTIFREEZE POISONING
Induce vomiting with hydrogen peroxide. Seek *immediate* veterinary help!

BLEEDING
Apply pressure above the area; treat wound by applying a cotton pack.

FISH HOOKS
Removal best handled by vet; hook must be cut in order to remove.

HEAT STROKE
Move animal to cool, shaded area, wet animal with water and place ice packs around head and body; seek immediate veterinary aid.

SNAKE BITES
Pack ice around bite; contact vet quickly; identify snake for proper antivenin.

FROSTBITE/HYPOTHERMIA
Warm the cat with a warm bath, electric blankets or hot water bottles.

ASPHYXIA
Cat must breathe fresh air as soon as possible. Encourage your cat to move around.

ABRASIONS
Clean the wound and wash out thoroughly with fresh water; apply antiseptic.

Remember: an injured cat may attempt to bite a helping hand from fear and confusion. Handle your cat in a calm and gentle manner so as to avoid upsetting the animal further.

THE GERIATRIC CAT

Depending on lifestyle, most cats are considered old at 12 years of age. Some problems that are associated with cats in their senior years are:

- Decreased energy
- Intolerance to heat and cold
- Less meticulous grooming and litter-box habits
- Decrease in mental alertness
- Decline of liver and kidney functions
- Greater susceptibility to diseases, especially dental disease
- Increased occurrence of cancer

As long as owners pay attention and adjust for changing behaviour and diet and continue regular veterinary care, cats can live well into their teens—some even 20 years and older!

WHAT TO DO WHEN THE TIME COMES

You are never fully prepared to make a rational decision about putting your cat to sleep. It is very obvious that you love your cat or you would not be reading this book. Putting a loved cat to sleep is extremely difficult. It is a decision that must be made with your veterinary surgeon. You are usually forced to make the decision when your beloved pet will only suffer more and experience no enjoyment for the balance of its life. Then euthanasia is the right choice.

How Old Is Your Cat Compared to You?

HUMAN'S AGE

CAT'S AGE

WHAT IS EUTHANASIA?

Euthanasia derives from the Greek meaning *good death*. In other words, it means the planned, painless killing of a cat suffering from a painful, incurable condition, or who is so aged that it cannot walk, see, eat or control its excretory functions.

Euthanasia is usually accomplished by injection with an overdose of an anaesthesia or barbiturate. Aside from the prick of the needle, the experience is usually painless.

MAKING THE DECISION

The decision to euthanise your cat is never easy. The days during which the cat becomes ill and the end occurs can be unusually stressful for you. If this is your first experience with the death of a loved one, you may need the comfort dictated by your religious beliefs. If you are the head of the family and have children, you should have involved them in the decision of putting your cat to sleep. Usually your cat can be maintained on drugs for a few days in order to give you ample time to make a decision. During this time, talking with members of your family or even people who have lived through this same experience can ease the burden of your inevitable decision.

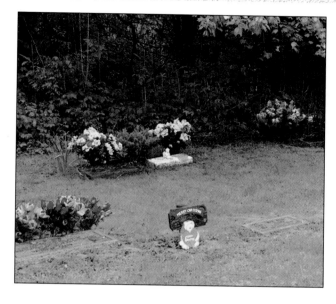

THE FINAL RESTING PLACE

Cats can have some of the same privileges as humans. The remains of your beloved cat can be buried in a pet cemetery, which is generally expensive. Cats who have died at home can be buried in your garden in a place suitably marked with some stone or newly planted tree or bush. Alternatively, they can be cremated individually and the ashes returned to you. A less expensive option is mass cremation, although, of course, the ashes can not then be returned. Vets can usually arrange the cremation on your behalf. The cost of these options should always be discussed frankly and openly with your veterinary surgeon.

The remains of your beloved cat can be buried in a pet cemetery.

HOMEOPATHY:
an alternative to conventional medicine

'Less is Most'

Using this principle, the strength of a homeopathic remedy is measured by the number of serial dilutions that were undertaken to create it. The greater the number of serial dilutions, the greater the strength of the homeopathic remedy. The potency of a remedy that has been made by making a dilution of 1 part in 100 parts (or 1/100) is 1c or 1cH. If this remedy is subjected to a series of further dilutions, each one being 1/100, a more dilute and stronger remedy is produced. If the remedy is diluted in this way six times, it is called 6c or 6cH. A dilution of 6c is 1 part in 1000,000,000,000. In general, higher potencies in more frequent doses are better for acute symptoms and lower potencies in more infrequent doses are more useful for chronic, long-standing problems.

CURING OUR CATS NATURALLY

Holistic medicine means treating the whole animal as a unique, perfect living being. Generally, holistic treatments do not suppress the symptoms that the body naturally produces, as do most medications prescribed by conventional doctors and vets. Holistic methods seek to cure disease by regaining balance and harmony in the patient's environment. Some of these methods include use of nutritional therapy, herbs, flower essences, aromatherapy, acupuncture, massage, chiropractic, and, of course the most popular holistic approach, homeopathy. Homeopathy is a theory or system of treating illness with small doses of substances which, if administered in larger quantities, would produce the symptoms that the patient already has. This approach is often described as 'like cures like.' Although modern veterinary medicine is geared toward the 'quick fix,' homeopathy relies on the belief that, given the time, the body is able to heal itself and return to its natural, healthy state.

Choosing a remedy to cure a problem in our cats is the difficult part of homeopathy. Consult with your veterinary surgeon for a professional diagnosis of your cat's symptoms. Often these symptoms require immediate conventional care. If your vet is willing, and somewhat knowledgeable, you may attempt a homeopathic remedy. Be aware that cortisone prevents homeopathic remedies from working. There are hundreds of possibilities and combinations to cure many problems in cats, from basic physical problems such as excessive moulting, fleas or other parasites, fever, severe skin problems, upset tummy, dry, oily or dull coat, diarrhoea, ear problems or eye discharge (including tears and dry or mucousy matter), to behavioural abnormalities, such as fear of loud noises, hypersensitivity to pain, poor appetite, aversion to touch, obesity and various phobias. From alumina to zincum metallicum, the remedies span the planet and the imagination…from flowers and weeds to chemicals, insect droppings, table salt and volcanic ash.

Using 'Like to Treat Like'

Unlike conventional medicines that suppress symptoms, homeopathic remedies treat illnesses with small doses of substances that, if administered in larger quantities, would produce the symptoms that the patient already has. While the same homeopathic remedy can be used to treat different symptoms in different cats, here are some interesting remedies and their uses.

Apis Mellifica
(made from honey bee venom) can be used for allergies or to reduce swelling that occurs in acutely infected kidneys.

Calcarea Fluorica
(made from calcium fluoride which helps harden bone structure) can be useful in treating hard lumps in tissues.

Kali Muriaticum
(made from potassium chloride) can help improve sluggish behaviour.

Natrum Muriaticum
(made from common salt, sodium chloride) is useful in treating thin, thirsty cats.

Nitricum Acidum
(made from nitric acid) is used for symptoms you would expect to see from contact with acids such as lesions, especially where the skin joins the linings of body orifices or openings such as the lips and nostrils.

Symphytum
(made from the herb Knitbone, *Symphytum officianale*) is used to encourage bones to heal.

Urtica Urens
(made from the common stinging nettle) is used in treating painful, irritating rashes.

USEFUL ADDRESSES

GREAT BRITAIN
The Governing Council of the Cat Fancy (GCCF)
4-6 Penel Orlieu, Bridgewater, Somerset, TA6 3PG
Email: GCCF_CATS@compuserve.com   Fax: 01278 446627 Tel: 01278 427575

The Cat Association of Britain (CA)
Mill House, Letcombe Regis, Oxon OX12 9JD   Tel: 01235-766-543

EUROPE
Federation Internationale Feline (FIFe)
Little Dene, Lenham Heath, Maidstone, Kent ME17 2BS, GB
Email: penbyd@compuserve.com   Fax: 1622 850193 Tel: 1622 850908

World Cat Federation (WCF)
Hubertsrabe 280, D-45307, Essen, Germany
Email: wcf@nrw-online.de   Fax: 201-552747 Tel: 201-555724

AUSTRALIA
The Australian Cat Federation, Inc. (ACF)
PO Box 3305, Port Adelaide, SA 5015
Email: acf@catlover.com   Fax: 08 8242 2767 Tel: 08 8449 5880

CANADA
Canadian Cat Association (CCA)
220 Advance Boulevard, Suite 101, Brampton, Ontario L6T 4J5
Email: office@cca-afc.com   Fax: 99050 459-4023 Tel: 99060459-1481

SOUTH AFRICA
Cat Federation of Southern Africa (CFSA)
PO Box 25, Bromhof 2154, Gauteng Province, Republic of South Africa

USA
American Cat Association (ACA)
8101 Katherine Avenue, Panorama City, CA 91402
Fax: (818) 781-5340 Tel: (818) 781-5656

American Cat Fanciers Association
PO Box 203, Point Lookout, MO 65726
Email: info@acfacat.com   Fax: (417) 334-5540 Tel: (417) 334-5430

Cat Fanciers Association, Inc. (CFA)
PO Box 1005, Manasquan, NJ 08736-0805
Email: cfa@cfainc.org   Fax: (732) 528-7391 Tel: (732) 528-9797

Cat Fanciers Federation (CFF)
PO Box 661, Gratis, OH 45330
Email: Lalbert933@aol.com Fax: 937-787-4290 Tel: (937) 787-9009

The International Cat Association (TICA)
PO Box 2684, Harlingen, TX 78551
Email: ticaeo@xanadu2.net Tel: (956) 428-8046

AACE: American Association of Cat Enthusiasts. A recently formed feline association in America.

ACF: Australian Cat Federation. Major Australian association that represents numerous cat registries.

Agouti: The ticked pattern created by alternate light/dark pigment banding seen along the hairs of a non-mutated cat's coat.

Altered: Cats that have been de-sexed.

ACA: American Cat Association. Oldest of the American registries.

Autosomal: Refers to body cells as opposed to sex (germ) cells.

Awn (bristle) hair: Those hairs that lie between the outer guard hairs of the coat and those that form the undercoat.

Bib: The chest area of the ruff in long and semi-longhaired cats.

Bi-colour: A pattern comprising a colour and white.

Blaze: A marking of colour, usually white, that extends down the nose.

Blood type incompatibility (BTI): Cats have two blood types: A and B. Type A is dominant to type B and is the most common. Type B mothers should never nurse a type A offspring, as this will prove fatal to the kitten.

Break: The area where the nose and forehead meet. Also called the stop.

Breast bone: Sternum.

Britches: The long hair on the back of the hind legs.

Burmese restriction: Refers to the gene that creates the Burmese pattern.

CA: The Cat Association of Britain. A cat registry and the British representative of the FIFe.

Calico: Alternative name for the tortoiseshell and white pattern.

Calling: The unmistakable sound of a female when she is in heat (oestrus) and calling to attract a male.

Cameo: Term given to the red or cream tipped hairs.

Canine teeth: The large paired fangs (dog teeth) of the upper and lower jaw.

Carpus bone: Wrist.

Cat flu: A common name that covers any of the many viruses that affect the respiratory system. Vaccines are available against some of these.

Catnip: Common name for the herb *Nepeta cataria*, whose scent cats find irresistible.

Cat registry: A feline ruling body that issues cat registrations, cat standards and, in general, administrates matters relating to cat show regulations and breed recognition.

Caudal vertebrae: Tail bones.

CCA: Canadian Cat Association. Canada's only feline registry. Administrates in both English and French languages.

CFA: Cat Fanciers Association. The main American registry—the world's largest.

CFF: Cat Fanciers Federation. American cat registry.

CFSA: Cat Federation of Southern Africa.

Champion: In Britain a cat that has won three Challenge Certificates under three different judges, at three different shows. In some countries, such as America, the system may vary and be based on acquiring a specific number of points.

Championship breed status: The final stage in full breed recognition. It can take many years to progress from preliminary to championship status.

Chinchilla: A coat pattern in which only the very tips of the hairs carry pigment, the rest of the hair being white or nearly so.

Chintz: Former name used in Britain for the tortoiseshell and white pattern.

Chromosome: One of paired thread-like structures found in the nucleus of all cells. They contain the genes that collectively determine all aspects of the cat.

Cleft Palate: A birth defect in which the bones of the hard palate do not develop correctly.

Cobby: A compact and sturdily built body.

Colostrum: The milk released by a female for two or three days after a kitten is born and which is rich in antibodies and protein.

Colourpoint: Terms used for the Siamese pattern when seen in other breeds.

Conformation: The way a cat's anatomy is arranged including its coat type, colour and overall appearance.

Congenital: Present from birth.

Counter conditioning: A psychological term for any stimuli that will weaken, stop or replace a given behavioural action.

Cystitis: Inflammation of the bladder caused by bacteria.

Dental formula: The number and type of teeth in a cat. *Adult:* I 3/3 C 1/1 PM 3/2 M 1/1= half jaw (upper/lower) x 2 = 30 *Kitten:* Same as adult, and deciduous, but no molars = 26

Dewclaw: The short toe and claw found on the inside of the front legs above the toes.

Dermatitis: Any of the various skin disorders often commonly called eczema.

Diarrhoea: Common term applied to the semi-liquid state of faecal matter that is the outward indicator of many internal disorders and diseases.

Digitigrade: Walking on the toes like a cat, as opposed to the feet (plantigrade) as in bears and man, or on the nails as in horses (unguiligrade).

Dominant gene: A mutant gene that needs to be present only in single dose to visually express itself.

Double coat: The presence of an obvious topcoat and a softer and dense underfur or coat.

Down hair: The short and soft hairs that create the heat retaining undercoat of a cat's fur.

Entire: A cat that still has its reproductive organs in tact. An unaltered cat.

GLOSSARY

Fading kitten syndrome: The condition where kittens die for no apparent reason, but often because of blood type incompatibility.

Feline calici virus (FCV): Respiratory disorder. A vaccine is available.

Feline dysautonomia: A rare disease of the nervous system also known as Key-Gaskell Syndrome. Permanently dilated pupils are amongst the indicators.

Feline immuno-deficiency virus (FIV): A disease of the white blood cells. No vaccine available.

Feline infectious anaemia (FIA): Disease caused by blood cell parasites transmitted by fleas and ticks.

Feline infectious enteritis (FIE): Disease of the digestive and blood systems. A vaccine is available. Also known as Feline panleukopenia.

Feline infectious peritonitis (FIP): Disease of the digestive and nervous systems: No vaccine available.

Feline leukaemia virus (FeLV): Highly infectious viral disease of the blood system. A vaccine is available.

Feline viral rhinotracheitis (FVR): Respiratory disorder, usually more serious than FCV. A vaccine is available.

Feline urological syndrome (FUS): The feline term for urolithiasis, a condition in which crystals form in the urinary tract.

Felis catus: Scientific name for the domestic cat.

Femur: Thigh bone.

FIFe: Federation Internationale Feline. A world federation of cat associations whose members apply common rules and regulations.

Flank: The area between the ribs and hips of a cat.

Foreign: Cats of a slim or lithe conformation. A group of such cats is in the classification of the GCCF.

GCCF: Governing Council of the Cat Fancy. Britain's largest, and the world's oldest, cat registry.

Gene: The unit of inheritance.

Genotype: The genetic make-up of one or more characteristics.

Gestation period: The time lapse between fertilisation and the birth of kittens, typically 63 days.

Gingivitis: A disease of the gums that results in bad breath, bad teeth and other maladies.

Ground colour: The basic colour in the tabby over which the pattern itself is superimposed.

Guard hairs: The stiff, coarse and long hairs that provide the outer protection to a cat's coat.

Haematoma: Blood blister in cats often found in the ear flap.

Heartbeat rate: In cats this should be 160-240 per minute.

Hereditary myopathy: A condition that negatively affects the muscles, causing problems in head carriage and walking difficulties.

Heterozygous: When each gene of a pair is for different expressions: non-pure-breeding for a given characteristic.

Himalayan: An alternative name for the colourpoint pattern in the Persian breed. In some American associations, it is regarded as a separate breed as the Persian.

Hip dysplasia: Disease of the hip characterised by excessive movement of the femoral head. Usually associated with the larger and heavier breeds.

Hock (ankle): Tarsus bone—the joint that receives the tibia or shin bone.

Homozygous: When both genes of a pair are of for the same expression: pure-breeding for a given characteristic.

Incisor teeth: The six small teeth situated between the canine teeth of each jaw.

Iris: The coloured area that surrounds the eye pupil.

Jacobson's organ: A highly sensitive organ situated in the roof of the mouth and which analyses tastes and smells. Associated with Flehming when cats, usually males, lift their upper lip to receive female scents.

Kitten: For show purposes in Britain a cat that is 14 or more weeks of age but under 9 months of age. In America the age is 16 weeks but under 8 months of age.

Locus: Genetic term for a gene's location along a chromosome (pl. loci).

Masking: Genetic term meaning the ability of a gene to suppress the effect of one or more other genes so that they are not visually apparent. The genetic name for this is epistasis.

Metacarpus bones: Front feet or paw.

Metatarsus bones: Hind feet or paw.

Milk fever (lactational tetany): Condition created in a nursing female through lack of blood calcium levels. Causes staggering and vomiting.

Moggie (Moggy): The old and still popular common name for a mongrel cat.

Molar teeth: The teeth behind the premolars.

Mutation: The change in the way a gene expresses itself visually or in its physiological functioning.

Muzzle: The jaws and mouth.

Neck bones: Cervical vertebrae.

Neuter class: A show class for cats that have been de-sexed.

Neutering: De-sexing. Castration in males—removal of testes. Spaying in females—removal of uterus and ovaries

Odd-eyed: White cats having one blue- and one orange-coloured eye.

pH value: A number used to denote the degree of acidity or alkalinity of a solution, neutral being seven. Values below this are acidic, above this alkaline. Cats require a urine pH of about 6 or just below this.

Pedigree: A document that indicates the line of descent. A moggie may have a pedigree as well as a pure-bred cat.

Pen (cage) judging: When cats are judged immediately outside their holding pen or cage.

Pet passport: A document that allows a cat to travel to and from Britain within the European Community without the need to be quarantined on its entry or return.

Pewter: A tipped pattern similar to the shaded silver, but where the eye colour is orange or copper, not green.

Phenotype: The visual expression of a gene—its appearance, i.e. longhair, rex coat, colour, pattern, etc.

Plasmocytic-lymphocytic stomatitis: Gingivitis, a gum disease.

Polydactyl: Having more than five toes on the front feet (including the dewclaw) and four on the hind feet.

Polygenic: When any given characteristic is determined by a number of genes rather than a pair.

Preliminary Breed Status: The first stage towards full breed recognition with the GCCF and other registries.

Premier: In cat shows the neutered cat's title, equivalent of a champion.

Premolars: The teeth behind the canine and in front of the molars.

Prepotent: Said of a cat of either sex that is able to consistently pass its type to its offspring, regardless of its mate's type. This is usually due to homozygosity of genotype.

Prolapse: A condition in which the uterus or rectum is pushed out of the body due to excess straining.

Provisional breed status: The second stage towards full breed recognition by the GCCF and some other registries.

Pulse rate: In cats this should be 160-240 per minute.

Pupil: The dark-coloured centre of the eye.

Queen: An unaltered female cat.

Quick: That part of the nail that contains a blood vessel.

Registration certificate: A document that records the birth date of a kitten, its immediate ancestry, and its breeder and owner.

Reinforcement: A psychological term for any external or internal stimuli that will encourage retention of any given action.

Recessive gene: A mutant gene that must be present in double dose before it is expressed visually.

Respiration rate: In cats this should be 20-30 per minute.

Ring judging: When cats are taken from their pens to be judged on a table.

Ringworm: A fungal infection of the skin.

Self-colour: A colour that is the same all over the body.

Sex chromosomes: Paired chromosomes of unequal length. One is designated as X while the shorter one is the Y. In mammals the male is XY and the female XX.

Sex-linked: Any trait found on the sex chromosomes and which link the sex to the trait. The colour red and its dilution, cream, are sex-linked colours and carried on the X chromosome.

Shaded: Tipped coat pattern midway between the chinchilla and the smoke.

Shoulder bone: Scapula.

Siamese restriction: Refers to the gene that creates the Siamese (colourpoint) coat pattern.

Smoke: Darkest of the tipped coat patterns.

Squint: When the eyes appear to be permanently looking at the nose—cross-eyed.

Sternum: Breastbone.

Stress: Subconscious fear or nervousness often difficult to identify. It reduces the effectiveness of the immune system and induces illness more rapidly, while slowing down recovery.

Tail bones: Caudal vertebrae.

Tarsus bone: Hock or ankle.

Taurine: An essential amino acid that can cause blindness in cats if it is deficient in the diet.

Temperature: The normal temperature for a healthy cat is between 38–39° C (100—102° F).

Thigh bone: Femur.

Third eyelid: Also known as the haw or nictitating membrane. Located in the corner of the eye, it is usually only seen clearly when the cat is unwell.

Threshold: A psychological term for the degree of stimulus required to elicit a response. A low threshold requires minimal stimulus.

TICA: The International Cat Association. One of the larger American registries.

TCA: Traditional Cat Association. American registry formed to cater to those wishing to preserve traditional forms of breeds such as the Persian and Siamese.

Tom: An unaltered male cat.

Trichobezoar: In veterinary language, this means hairballs.

Tri-colour: An alternative name for the tortoiseshell and white. A three-colour pattern comprising two pigment colours and white.

Vetting in: The veterinary examination of each cat before it is allowed into a show venue. Not always a requirement outside the UK.

WCF: World Cat Federation. German-based organisation with member registries in a few other countries, notably Brazil.

Whisker break: The area immediately behind the whisker pads.

Zoonoses: Diseases that can be passed between animals and humans.

Zygote: The fertilised egg (ovum) from which the organism will develop.

INDEX

My Ragdoll Cat

PUT YOUR KITTEN'S FIRST PICTURE HERE

Kitten's Name _____

Date _____ Photographer _____

Birth Date _____

Origin (Breeder's Name) _____

Breeder's Address _____ Phone _____

Registration/I D Number _____

Distinguishing Features _____

IN CASE OF LOST CAT

Vet's Name _____

Vet's Address _____ Phone _____

VACCINATION RECORD	
VACCINE	DATES